Astrological Insights into the Spiritual Life

Dane Rudhyar
A Seed Man

Dane Rudhyar was born in Paris, France on March 23, 1895.

Quite early in his life, Rudhyar intuitively came to realize two things which have deeply influenced his entire life and work: (1) Time is cyclic, and the Law of Cycles describes all civilizations as well as all existence; (2) Western Civilization is now in what could be symbolically called the autumn phase of its period of existence. As these realizations developed into a personal commitment to the future which he envisioned, Rudhyar felt the urge to divorce himself from Europe and to seek a "New World" — a land into which he could, as it were, sow himself as a seed, carrying within his being the legacy of whatever was viable and constructive in the European past. In the late fall of 1916, he came to America, leaving behind his native land and ancestral French culture as well as his family name, Chenneviere.

The change of name was symbolic of a total dedication to his ideal: the transformation of our civilization, a 'revaluation of all values.' He became known as 'Rudhyar,' a name derived from the Sanskrit root *rudra* implying dynamic action and the electrical power released during storms. The god *Rudra* in the *Vedas* is the Destroyer and Regenerator, the transforming energy, breaker of old molds and the power of will or vital force.

This sense of destiny released through Rudhyar tremendous energy which he has channeled into the development of his philosophical ideas; through Music and the use of Tone; through Painting as the Art of Gestures; through Astrology as a symbolic language with the potential to bring individuals in tune with cosmic cycles. Throughout his long life and his use of many different forms of expression, his purpose has become ever more clearly focused and dynamic. He calls forth the need for individuals with holistic vision and a 'transpersonal' approach to life to serve as the foundation of a global society.

March 23, 1895 – September 13, 1985

Astrological Insights into the Spiritual Life

by
Dane
Rudhyar

drawings by Judge
from the original pencil
sketches by Rudhyar 1938

AURORA PRESS
P.O. BOX 573, SANTA FE, NEW MEXICO 87504

To our California friends
who became fascinated by
the lore of the sky.

Aurora Press, Inc.
P.O. Box 573
Santa Fe, N.M. 87504
Printed in the United States of America

Library of Congress Cataloging in Publication Data

Rudhyar, Dane, 1895-
    Astrological insights.

    1. Zodiac.   I. Title.
BF1726.R8   133.5'2   79-1210
ISBN:0-943358-09-4

Contents

Introduction

During the Summer, 1938 while living in Santa Fe, New Mexico, I found myself close to several painters who had felt the need of forming an officially recognized group because they were all sharing an approach to Art definitely different from the more fashionable trends highly publicized in the big cities of the East Coast. I participated in their discussion and their search for a name, and they finally adopted my suggestion, calling their group the Transcendental Painting Group. At that time, a great deal of attention was being given to the philosophers and authors who, a century before, had been known as the New England Transcendentalists — Emerson, Thoreau, Hawthorne and the Alcotts. So the name seemed particularly apt, as it also pointed to the sprirtual orientation shared by all my painter friends, though their works differed greatly from one another's in technique and style.

A year later a Transcendental Painting Foundation was organized (of which I became Vice-President), in order to promote the ideals of the group. Included in the group were Lawren Harris (President of the Foundation), Raymond Jonson, Agnes Pelton, and Emil Bisttram.*

I did not belong to the Transcendental Painting group itself because at the time I had done no painting or drawing; but for a number of years, my musical career had been blocked by the antagonism of Neo-Classicists who since the late Twenties had come to control all openings in the music world, and being stimulated by

---

*Remarkable examples of what could be also called transcendental art are now to be found in the book *Cosmic Art* by Raymond F. and Lila K. Piper, edited by Ingo Swann and published by Hawthorn Books, N.Y. (1975). Reproductions of paintings by Emil Bisttram and Agnes Pelton are included, and an early drawing (1938) of mine, "Avatar."

my painter friends and that summer living in favorable conditions in Santa Fe, I felt the urge to draw and eventually to paint. This, I felt, would somewhat take the place of music in my creative life.

As a book of my poems, **White Thunder,** was being published in a limited deluxe edition, beautifully bound by the nationally-known art-binder, Hazel Dreis, I decided to make a pen and ink drawing entitled **Storm Gods** to be used as a frontispiece for the book.†

Encouraged by the result and my friends' appreciative comments, I began a series of pencil sketches using the traditional forms associated with the twelve zodiacal signs as a starting point. I entitled the series **Zodiacal Signatures** and showed it to Raymond Jonson, a prolific and extremely gifted non-representational painter who I had known for a few years. He was impressed by the sketches and asked if he might use them as a basis for a set of twelve fairly large size painting. Talking about the idea, it occurred to me that they could make a beautiful album, and that I could write some poetic lines referring to each zodiacal sign to accompany the reproduction of the paintings.

Raymond Jonson approved of the idea, and produced the paintings during the following year. After the Transcendental Painting Foundation was organized during the Summer, 1939, we thought the album might sooner or later be published by the Foundation. That summer, I also wrote a book, **The Transcendental Movement in the Arts,** which dealt not only with the Transcendental Painting group, but also with other kinds of recent artistic manifestations, including the modern dance which Martha Graham and others were developing in a striking manner.

Unfortunately the War begin on September 1, 1939. The response of Eastern galleries and critics to the announcement of the formation of the Transcendental Painting group and Foundation, and to a small booklet we issued and circularized at the time, was a resounding silence or lack of interest. The war separated

---

†Seed Center, 1976 Palo Alto, Ca.

4

some of the members of the Group, and eventually, a few years after the war, the Foundation was dissolved, having accomplished nothing. Raymond Jonson exhibited some of the paintings following very closely my original sketches; but he eventually forgot having seen these sketches. So much happened in my life that I also had almost forgotten these first attempts, which later were followed by paintings of various kinds and black and white drawings.

A year or so ago, I happened to come upon the zodiacal sketches I had pasted in an album and my interest in them was revived. I showed the sketches, now partly faded, to some friends who urged me to publish them in a better form. As I had not been drawing or painting for many years, being totally occupied by writing and revising numerous books — and dealing with publishers at last willing to bring them out — I realized that it would not be possible for me to re-do the drawings. I showed them to Judge, suggesting to him that he might like to finish and, wherever needed, somewhat develop them. He enthusiastically accepted the suggestion, and a few copies of his drawings and the poetic lines I had written for them in Palo Alto in February 1976 were privately printed.

At the suggestion of Henry Weingarten and Barbara Somerfield, I have added to the material two articles covering related zodiacal themes in what I believe is a deeply symbolic yet practical way. These articles were first published in Popular Library Magazines,* and they have been revised and edited by Leyla Rael, to whom I extend my thanks for this work.

Palo Alto
August, 1978

---

*"The Zodiac, Giver of Life" appeared in two parts in Zodiac Magazine, August and September, 1971. "Twelve Qualities Required for the Spiritual Life" was published January 1972.

The Life Giving Zodiac and Its 12 Great Gifts

The Life-Giving Zodiac and Its Twelve Great Gifts

Ever since popular magazines on astrology reached the general public, readers have learned that when they were born, the Sun was found in one of the twelve signs of the zodiac, and that this was in some sense *their* sign. As a result, they could be expected to have certain traits of character as well as more or less definite features and/or physiological characteristics. Yet, even people who have had an astrologer calculate and interpret their individual birth-charts according to the exact time and place of birth would, in most cases, find it difficult to explain clearly and convincingly what the zodiac actually is, why it is divided into twelve "signs," and what is precisely meant by the "entrance" of the sun, or of a planet, into a zodiacal sign.

To make matters worse, if the reader of magazines or books on astrology diligently sought knowledge concerning the above-mentioned questions, he would soon realize that even "authorities" disagree on many important points. Yet underlying the differences of opinions is a basis of agreement insofar as the *idea* of the zodiac is concerned. Differences occur primarily in relation to how to apply the idea to astronomical facts and to matters dealing with the existence of human beings. What I shall try to clarify in the following is the idea of the zodiac, that is, the basic reason for believing that nearly everything in life can be explained or significantly interpreted by referring human experiences and individual character to the celestial entity we call the zodiac.

Many years ago, I wrote a series of articles entitled "The Universal Matrix" which referred to the zodiac.* The word, matrix, gives the main clue to the reason for the idea that our

*Now published in paperback as *Astrological Signs: The Pulse of Life* (Sham-Shala Publication; Boulder, Colorado: 1970)

planet, Earth, is surrounded by some kind of celestial "envelope" or field of electro-magnetic activity which in the Western world we call the zodiac. Every living organism exists within some sort of electro-magnetic field; it takes form and acquires substantial existence within that field somewhat as an embryo develops within the mother's enfolding womb after conception.

The zodiac can therefore be considered a kind of "matrix" — or a cosmic egg — within which our entire planet, and particularly its biosphere (the realm of life on and around the Earth's surface) develops its myriads of life-forms. The zodiac supplies these life-forms with the energies they require for their very existence and growth.

However, as far as our modern scientific knowledge goes, the energies which reach the Earth do not *originate* in the zodiac. They emanate from the Sun. Still, there are astrologers who claim — if they are consistent in their ideas — that these energies *do* originate in what they call the sidereal zodiac, that is in a group of constellations of stars. They believe that the Sun acts only as the fountainhead or source of these energies. Water actually does not flow from a fountainhead or source; it flows *through* it. It surges from the depth of the soil and only emerges at the point called its source. It could be that the Sun is like a lens, or in another sense, an electrical transformer. Cosmic zodiacal energies would be released *through* the Sun, but not generated within the Sun.

If one accepts such a cosmic picture, one has therefore to believe that the zodiac is a vast galactic sphere enveloping the entire solar system, divided into constellations of stars far beyond the outermost limits of our solar system. This concept, however, does not fit in well with what we know about solar energies and their effect upon the Earth's biosphere; and it is far simpler and more practical to think of the zodiac as the Earth's aura, that is, as a quasi-spherical field surrounding our globe. But what does this field really represent?

Modern astronomy as well as man's common experiences of light and warmth tell us that the energies which reach our biosphere and all its living organisms originate in the Sun. They radiate through the entire solar system; and as within this system a number of planets (plus planetoids, comets, etc.) move at various speeds, the whole solar system is filled with an immense variety of direct solar energies and secondary waves produced by the motions of all celestial bodies within that system. All these waves hit the Earth's ionosphere (and other-spheres far above the surface of the globe), and the result is indeed very complex in terms of electromagnetic phenomena — some of which modern science knows today, but perhaps many others as yet unknown.

If the zodiac is a matrix or "auric egg" surrounding the Earth, all the energies circulating within the solar system must pass through it before reaching the ionosphere and biosphere. Therefore, we should not primarily think of the zodiac as a field of forces, but as something of a different nature. Let us rather picture the zodiac as a field of *potentialities of existence* — or, we may also say, of archetypes.

The zodiac refers to what some occult philosophies spoke of as the World of Formation; and in ancient times the twelve zodiacal signs were thought of as Creative Hierarchies. In those days — often referred to as the Vitalistic Ages — religions centered around the worship of the Life-force in its bi-polar (male-female) aspects. Fertility cults existed on all continents, and many still exist today in more or less modified forms — for instance among the Pueblo Indians of the Southwest, throughout Africa and some Asiatic countries. The Sun and Moon were considered the cosmic sources of the bi-polar Life-force, and this force was supposed to be focused in the sign of the zodiac in which these two "Lights" were located at any time.

In other words, as the solar radiations passed through a zodiacal sign, for instance Aries, these rays aroused and mobilized the *potentialities of concrete organic existence inherent in Aries.* Stated in archaic terms, the Aries hierarchy of divine Intelligences became mobilized for action as the Sun poured its energy through their special realm, and whatever was born (or occurred) then on this Earth became impressed with the specific type of organic, biological and psychic features and characteristics of which the Aries hierarchy was the cosmic model or archetype.

What the Sun radiated into space, the Moon, as it circled around the Earth, distributed to all living beings according to their particular needs at the time. Each year the Sun journeyed across, and thus mobilized, the whole zodiacal field, the twelve Powers inherent in this field. Since there are normally twelve New Moons in a year, and one in every zodiacal sign, each New Moon was specifically associated with one of the twelve hierarchies and their archetypes. At these New Moons, the Sun impregnated the Moon with its most powerful Ray (the *Sushumna* Ray in Hindu occultism), and the creative imagination of the hierarchy related to the zodiacal sign in which this New Moon occurred was stirred most deeply, projecting a special image of power into the higher psychic realms of the Earth. This image grew in effectiveness as the Moon waxed, and at Full Moon man was theoretically able to perceive this great image, consciously, using it thereafter as a guiding symbol in his activities.

The concept of celestial hierarchies may seem very archaic and obsolete in these days of modern science, even though it has also been used in a slightly different manner in our Christian religion. But if we think of it as a form of symbolism, we can still find a very fruitful use for the old imagery. Let us say that a person intrigued by what he read about astrology decides to study a textbook stating what the zodiac means. He will find listed under each sign a long series of traits of character, tendencies, physical and psychological features, etc. These lists may confuse the student, because they deal with what to the novice often appears to be unrelated and disconcerting. If he merely tries to memorize these attributes of each sign, his mind will be filled with heterogeneous and disconnected data. He will not see a truly valid and vital picture of what the nature of each sign really means.

The student can only gain a significant understanding of what the zodiac and its twelve signs represent and of *how to use* what he has learned from the text-book if he realizes that *a central quality of being* stands underneath the diversity of characteristics listed for each sign. From this one basic quality of being, many secondary and tertiary traits of behavior, feeling and thinking can be derived; and it is these which are listed, often in a rather haphazard or even incongruous manner, in astrological textbooks. But these traits have very little basic meaning unless one can refer and relate them to the one basic quality which the sign represents, or some will say, expresses.

The modern astrologer actually thinks of Aries, Taurus, Gemini, etc. very much as entities with a very specific character — which is not too different from seeing them as "divine hierarchies"! A hierarchy was, after all, only a class of intelligences, a class related to other classes which altogether constituted the Universal Mind. The zodiac-as-a-whole represented this Universal Mind in action; and the power that sequentially mobilized these twelve classes was essentially the Sun, the symbol of cosmic Life or divine Will.

As we deal with the zodiacal signs and their meanings, the essential point is that they are all different aspects of the one zodiac, just as the ancient celestial hierarchies were understood to be different aspects of the one Universal Mind, often identified with Space itself — but Space, not as mere emptiness, but rather as a fullness of cosmic being. Modern astronomy is at last coming to realize that interplanetary and interstellar spaces are filled with all kinds of vibrations and even substances.

Thus the student of astrology should realize that anything and everything said about any one particular zodiacal sign *must* have meaning in terms representing one particular phase, or aspect, of the entire cycle of existence and the fullness of being represented by the *zodiac-as-a-whole*. The zodiac is a complete whole. Its twelve signs are component parts of that whole; each of them is related to all the others. A zodiacal sign is particularly related to the sign opposite it, and to those which are at right angles to it, because the zodiac is essentially a symbolic-cosmic representation of *all* the possibilities of life on this Earth, and the life-force is basically bi-polar. Polarity is the most essential principle of existence — at least of existence as we know it. No one can understand the zodiac and its signs if he or she does not grasp the meaning of this polarization — a polarization which operates at several levels: atomic, biological, psychic, mental, cosmic.

The Yin-Yang Polarities

One of the most well-known and indeed most significant ways of symbolizing this universal principle of polarity today is the Chinese system expounded in Taoism in which the two life-polarities are called *Yin* (feminine) and *Yang* (masculine). If one applies it to the cycle produced by the annual (apparent) motion of the Sun around the whole sky — the cycle of the year — one can speak of these two polarities as the Day-Force and the Night-Force. These terms refer to the obvious fact that, at least in the temperate zones of the Earth, the lengths of the day and the night constantly vary during the year. At the spring equinox (which astrology today considers the beginning of "Nature's year") day and night are of equal length. Thereafter, the length of the day increases and that of the night decreases until the summer solstice when days are as long as they can be. As the days begin to decrease in length the nights become longer, equality is reached at the fall equinox and the nights are the longest at the winter solstice. Then the nights become gradually shorter and the days longer until they are the same length at the spring equinox; and the yearly cycle begins once more.

The Day-Force is the Chinese principle, Yang; the Night-Force is Yin. These two forces or principles are always and everywhere in existence. Neither one can entirely overcome the other; but at every moment of the year *their relative strengths* vary. These variations can be related to the seasonal activity of the Life-principle, and particularly to the annual cycle of vegetation in temperate climates. At the equator the Day-Force and the Night-Force are constantly equal, if we consider the lengths of days and nights; and at the poles there are only one long day and one long night every year. But astrology, as we know and use it today, was born and developed in temperate regions above the tropics. In the tropical-equatorial and the polar zones of our globe, life has a very different character and value.

Indeed astrology as practiced today basically refers to the state of mind related to human beings whose consciousness and way of life have been molded by cultures and religions developed in the temperate regions of the *northern* hemisphere of the Earth. Civilization may indeed always originate in the northern hemisphere, and if we look carefully at a map of the world we will see that most of the land is distributed north of the equator. The two great continental masses, the Americas and what I called Eurasiafrica, end southward in shapes suggesting down-pointing triangles, and thus a flow of energy from north to south. The exception, Australia and the islands around it, is probably the remnant of a continent which was linked with Antarctica, and which belonged to another geological and human Age. It is also probable that at the close of each of these Ages the Earth-poles are reversed, so that what is now north of the equator, may at another time be south of it. The equator itself most likely also changes location.

In summation, the zodiac represents the vast sphere of potentialities surrounding whatever achieves the status of an organic whole. In a sense, there is a zodiac around every living organism — and, according to ancient thought, every planet is or has been a living organism, and so is the solar system as a whole, and every galaxy. But "life" can operate at different levels and in an immeasurable diversity of ways. Every form of life, every organic whole, is surrounded by a complex set of potentialities, a zodiac. A living organism may or may not be able to actualize all these potentialities; but they are there around it.

In many fairytales we are told of a baby prince or princess who was surrounded at birth by a number of fairies each one bringing a special gift. In a similar sense every sign of the zodiac brings to the new organism the sum-total of archetypal possibilities which this organism *can* actualize according to the state of evolution of the life-species to which it belongs. Some of these

16

possibilities are *accentuated* by the fact that the Sun, the Moon and the planets are in some of the signs. The sign of the zodiac through which the Sun is passing at birth reveals the basic possibility of life-operation for the organism. It refers, as it were, to the "fuel" which the engine of personality will predominantly and most easily use in order to run — thus, to one of the twelve fundamental types of possibilities of existence in that particular life.

The "fuel" has to be properly distributed to all the parts of the engine; and the distributing agency is shown in astrology by the Moon. The planets refer to more complex factors in the operation of the personality. But the Sun, Moon and planets essentially mobilize and actualize the fundamental potentialities or organic existence symbolized by the zodiac. A person's essential nature is represented by the *pattern of mobilization* produced by the angular relationships among the ten planets (including now as planets the Sun and the Moon). This pattern reveals the manner in which the person *should* act, feel and think — in order to actualize in *his or her own individual way* potentialities which are inherent in human nature.

The Signs of the Zodiac

There are two great moments in the year's cycle of vegetation: the moment when the life within the seed is aroused and germination occurs, and the moment when the seed leaves the plant and falls into the ground, the promise of a future vegetation even as everything around it begins to disintegrate. These two great moments occur respectively at the spring and fall equinoxes, and are symbolized by the signs Aries and Libra.

Two other great moments of the yearly cycle are the summer solstice, which occurs at Cancer 0°, and the winter solstice — Capricorn 0°. Cancer represents symbolically the reconstitution of the seed within the flower, and Capricorn, the possibility of a new creative mutation within the seed hidden in the ground, perhaps under the protective covering of snow.

Of course all plants do not grow, mature and die, re-seeding themselves at the close of their annual cycle of existence according to this exact fourfold pattern of development; but the yearly process of vegetation is a potent symbol of what occurs *archetypally* in every physical organism. Other, more complex types of symbolism are needed to interpret and give meaning to other levels of existence. In the broadest possible sense, we can say that every cycle begins in and according to the quality of the zodiacal sign Aries. It reaches its *outer* fulfillment in Cancer. In Libra a new process begins which deals with *inner* or body-transcending values or mental qualities of existence. In Capricorn these values and qualities are fulfilled. And, as no fulfillment can or should be considered ultimate — for what has been fulfilled inevitably leaves much that is unachieved or that must be transcended — all achievements prove to be ephemeral. They become empty of meaning, and eventually disintegrate, as the new creative impulse asserts itself.

Aries

The essential potentiality or quality of existence represented by Aries is the ability to *spring into action*. The word mobilization may be used here as a keyword. Mobilization in the old-fashioned military sense means calling men away from their stable homes and businesses into a new type of outward-directed action.

Mobilization starts a process which has two main phases. The first is characterized by a breaking away from the past condition of stability, with all it may imply of "tearing oneself away," of fear of the future, of re-orientation of life's drives, and at the same time perhaps of ebullient and emotional enthusiasm, even if what one is enthusiastic about is not at all clear and its consequences hardly understood. The second phase implies action of a definite nature — that is, a direct meeting with the realities essential to the new situation. Militarily speaking, this means combat; more generally, dynamic encounter or engagement. There is no more looking back.

In order to spring into action, one has to spring from some relatively stable foundation or base of operation. This represents the past. No cycle begins without a past, and the unfinished business of the past largely conditions what the new activity will be. Thus the Aries type of person experiences the pull of the past, even through his eagerness to forge ahead. This may bring a special sense of insecurity, a fear of advancing too far or too emotionally lest one's base for action be left behind at an unreachable distance. This is usually true of the first decanate (ten degrees) of the sign Aries. In the last decanate the "springing into action" may be more assured, the will more secure, the assuming of responsibility more definite in terms of clearer goals. The Day-Force — the will to self-actualization — has by then increased its preponderance over the Night-Force which, as we shall see, refers mainly to collective factors and the drive toward some stable form of collective living and sharing.

Taurus

The keywords of this second phase of the zodiacal life-process are possessiveness and fertilization. The possibility *to own* what one needs in order further to actualize oneself is symbolized by Taurus; and ownership generates a certain kind of bondage, or at least of temporary limitation. Ownership gives stability and substantiality to the Aries drive for action, but it also "settles" this drive by defining its main sphere of action. The straight-forward, centrifugal motion of Aries becomes in Taurus a whirling circular movement reaching to and yearning for the possession of a particular center or core. Possessions prove the worth of an individual's mode of activity. "To be" acquires power in terms of "to have." In Gemini the drive will be in the direction of "to expand" in order to insure what one has. In Cancer, the motto will be "to hold"; in Leo, "to express"; in Virgo, "to improve." Each species of life seeks possession in its own way and according to its own needs.

A human being's needs for ownership vary with his degree of emotional, mental and spiritual maturity. A male usually wants to possess a female; a female, to possess a child. Possessiveness may be psychic — or even mental and "spiritual" — as well as physical. A leader seeks security in a fascinated following; many gurus *need* their chelas in order to exercise their fertilizing power at the pyschic level. The consciousness of man progresses from level to level of ownership. Man's fecundating power seeks ever more subtle and extensive substances to provide materials adequate for ever more inclusive and finer forms of self-actualization. The possibility of progressing in such a manner is the gift of Taurus to mankind.

♊
Gemini

The third sign of the zodiac is often associated with the will to know and to experience in terms of the possibilities offered by ever more extensive environments. A vivid extension of the capacity for relationship results from the potentiality, inherent in man, of adapting himself to a great variety of environments providing a multiplicity of sensations and encounters. Through complex relationships, an equally complex nervous system and multi-directional brain-processes are formed. Thus the feeling of ownership spreads out to include a great diversity of objects — physical or intellectual. What we call the concrete or lower mind is the mind able to possess, classify and interpret for personal use the results of sensations, meetings and fecundant relationships.

The intellect builds concepts and generalizes them into systems or theories *in order to possess knowledge.* It is an instrument for possession, and the basic tool it uses is, of course, "memory." One possesses mentally what one remembers clearly. The remembered data are like a harem; the women are available at any time for the use of the sultan — ego. This is why people — whether they be theologians, sociologists or scientists — often cling so tenaciously to their dogmas and theories. The clinging may not be exactly a Gemini trait, at least not an *early* Gemini trait; but as Gemini comes close to Cancer and thus to the summer solstice and the apex of the power of the Day-Force, the tendency to change the ever-widening spiral (the typical Gemini pattern) into a helicoidal circuit (which refers to Cancer) gains in strength. The possessor and the possessed stabilize their relationship on a basis of conjugal and fruitful exclusivity.

Cancer

The summer solstice represents the triumph of *the particular and the exclusive.* The living organism holds to its possessions in an individualized way and stamps them with definite characteristics. Matter is fecundated by spirit or the focused will of the ego-centered individual person. Thus Cancer symbolizes the possibility of establishing not only a secure and stable home, but first of all a more or less unique personality with a rhythm and character truly its own.

In Aries, activity is impelled by a superpersonal drive. It may be the unconscious urge to fulfill some past karma or the super-conscious and intuitive eagerness to act as the agent of some collective or planetary purpose; but whatever happens essentially occurs *through* the person, using the body as well as the mind as a channel. In Cancer, it is the ego, with all its complexes, which more or less consciously or deliberately is the actor. Action is focused by the ego's (or the body's) need and determined by the particular character of this need at a particular time and place. In Cancer man seeks to adjust himself to his environment so that he can operate as securely and happily as possible; and to this end he uses his inherent intelligence guided by his Gemini type of memory and thinking — that is, thinking related to particular and concrete situations. At the lowest level this means primitive cunning, and in a higher sense, the empirical and analytical approach of the scientific intellect.

♌
Leo

Like Aries, Leo is a zodiacal sign which has the attributes of what occult tradition understands as Fire. But while this element Fire in its Aries aspect refers to a universal process which operates regardless of particular conditions — it burns whatever it touches — the Leo type of Fire is the expression of an individually conscious will to burn, determined and directed by a particular purpose or need. Whatever the individual person possesses and can use is brought to a state of at least relative incandescence. It is "expressed" (i.e. forced outward) in order to "impress" the character and will of the individual upon all those who are impressionable. The Leo potentiality is therefore, in this sense, that of projecting one's image upon one's environment; and this is what is called "creativity."

Creativity may evidently operate at various levels, unconscious as well as conscious. The procreation of children occurs at the biological level and often indeed without conscious intent. However, creativity at the personal and social levels — and this of course includes the process of leadership in various fields — may often be a means to hide a sense of inferiority or a deeply rooted uncertainty. When one feels exposed, one may react by attacking. When one finds it difficult to meet people in an open way of sharing, one may try to overwhelm them by projecting one's own attainments or dreams upon them. The Leo type has recourse to great dramatic gestures whenever he feels uncertain of his ability to meet others in simple terms. He therefore often uses glamor, even if he is not ready to admit that he does. Indeed it may be difficult for him truly to cooperate with others.

If he accepts subservience and the role of the devotee, it is fundamentally — though he may not be aware of this — in order to identify himself with some great Image or purpose on the basis of which he will eventually be able to radiate outward his own interpretation and understanding. He is often most generous and noble — which accounts for the usual glorification of the sign Leo in astrology — but he is so because he has to feel himself generous and noble in order to operate in society in a self-satisfying way, i.e. in order to boost his own self-image. The creator must therefore perform great and generous deeds so that the image he sees in mirroring eyes will be beautiful and self-exalting.

Virgo

Self-expression, even if it is most glorifying in other people's eyes, most often leaves a residuum of dissatisfaction in the end. It may lead to failure. Man, of all living organisms, is perhaps the only one who can really learn, as an individual from his failure or sense of emptiness even in the midst of a worshipping crowd. Man can *improve* himself, through humiliation and perhaps illness if not through retraining and discipleship. He can be more than he is, even if he is a self-sufficient and proud ego. The crucial question is: when will he take the first step toward radical self-improvement and self-transformation — or will the step be forced upon him because the ground under his feet is collapsing? Our entire Western society has the ground collapsing under its feet, especially since the harsh conjunctions of Uranus and Pluto in Virgo in 1965-66. But its leaders and the bulk of the population refuse to acknowledge this. Sooner or later they will have to experience, in sorrow, what they could have learned in humility.

Virgo symbolizes the possibility to learn and transform oneself through a personal crisis — which may mean a catharsis. The word "crisis" etymologically means the possibility to make a decision (from *krino,* to decide). A decision is the act of accepting to become different from what one has been — thus the acceptance of change and self-transformation. The critic is the person who is able to see what could or should be changed in whatever has at least partially failed to actualize its inherent function or purpose. A critical person is one who tends to see what others should do to change themselves, yet he often uses this attitude as a mask to hide his own failure to change himself.

Libra

The first half of the zodiac refers to all the basic types of possibilities involved in the development of the human being primarily as an individual person. This person is of course living in some sort of environment and dealing with the other organisms and personalities he meets in it: but what he is basically concerned with is his own individual person and thus mainly his ego. Even as he radiates love for others, this love is essentially an overflow of energy which had to find some outer expression, or the expression of an inner dependence upon a person or object guaranteeing him needed security and rootedness. In Libra, a new type of possibility emerges which from then on will dominate the life-stage: the possibility to enter into a fruitful relationship with another person, or a group of persons, in order to generate consciousness and power at a new and individual-transcending level of existence.

This possibility already exists in the animal kingdom; but in man the social sense reaches its full expression, because man is capable of communicating *and recording* his experiences, thoughts and feelings by means of very complex sets of symbols. These records (words, works of art, institutionalized procedures and responses to life) can be transmitted from generation to generation, and a lasting culture and body of knowledge can thus be built. Libra refers to anything which contributes to the building of such a culture based on a social consciousness in which all the members of a community (small or large) may share.

As popularly supposed, Libra has actually nothing to do with "balance"! The symbol of the Scales refers to the procedure by which an individual's contribution to his community is *weighed* — i.e. measured and evaluated according to a collectively accepted standard of value. If anything is "balanced" it is, on the one hand, the desire of the individual to participate in a community which promises him a vaster scope for his activity, and on the other hand, his persisting will to remain an autonomous individual ego, a master in his own house.

Libra and the fall equinox reveal that the fundamental individualism in every man has become challenged by a force of equal power, i.e. the desire to be more than one can be as a single person by joining with others in true cooperation and sharing of consciousness and feeling-responses. The Night-Force now equals in strength the previously dominant Day-Force. This Night-force increases its power until Capricorn is reached, the apex of the socializing urge. If Libra refers to the arts and to love it is because art is the crystallization of social patterns of fellowship, and "the love of the companions" is the essence of unrestricted sharing and of the availability of each to all.

Scorpio

To *act* together is not enough. Companions should *feel* together and experience their togetherness at all levels, including that of the very depths of their bio-psychic and emotional natures. Scorpio reveals the possibility open to all human beings to surrender their individualized beings and their cherished egos to the experience of total relatedness and therefore of at least temporary identification with others.

The most basic experience of union today is the result of the sexual act, when its fulfillment obliterates the basic urge of the ego to remain "separate." But sexual fulfillment can, and usually does, produce a twofold or polarized kind of exclusiveness and individualization. This is natural and necessary at the level of purely biological functioning, when sex has a strictly procreative purpose and the forthcoming child needs a close focus of attention. But this refers to the sign Taurus, and *not* to Scorpio, whatever most astrologers may believe. Scorpio is a *social and psychological,* not a biological symbol. It does not deal with procreation, but with the possibility of human beings, each of whom has a definitely developed ego, to transcend, dissolve, or shatter their ego-separativeness in moments of unitive feeling — or even of passionate conflict.

This may occur through a rich sexual experience, but it can also occur at a somewhat more socialized level in group-rituals or group-meditation. There are many types of group-rituals, from a baseball or boxing spectacle which generates powerful collective excitement to a Catholic mass or any truly efficacious ceremonial performance along Occult lines. Included also are Nazi or Revivalist mass-meetings, or battlefields on which fellowship and solidarity may take on a heroic character and the bloods of adversaries may mix.

Lonely, tense or distraught egos may so long to experience moments of self-forgetting into another, and anxious intellects to lose themselves in an intensity of all-pervasive emotion, that the shadow of such longings is the particular type of possessiveness and jealousy associated with sexual passion. The ideal commune, of which many young people dream today, can only operate harmoniously where this possessiveness is overcome and the group life accepts the ritualization of some of its most profound emotional experiences.

Sagittarius

The more complex the cooperative activities of human beings become the greater the need for regulatory principles of social behavior, thus for definite patterns of order. When the power of the enitre collectivity is made ready so that these patterns are respected, a system of laws is built. As enforcement-mechanisms develop, the concept of the State takes precise form. Sagittarius refers to the possibility for man to think in terms of general principles regulating behavior — whether the behavior is being considered is of men in a close community, or the behavior of atoms, molecules and glands in a biological unit, the body. These principles have to be made not only acceptable, but convincing to the individual mind; thus philosophical and metaphysical-religious explanations are formulated. Without them a community is too open to the centrifugal power of individual devices and beliefs. A norm or standard has to be produced to test the validity of individuals' actions and thoughts, and even the worth of feeling-responses. Logic and ethics develop in this Sagittarian field.

The *abstract and generalizing* mind (Sagittarius) deals with collectively experienced and useful principles to which every member of a community is expected to give obedience. The formulation of these principles may change as time goes on, but the change must have the consent of the community as a whole, or at least of a specialized group. The change should reflect a corresponding transformation in the whole society — in its needs, its basic feeling-responses and its mentality. In contrast, the *concrete and individualized* mind (Gemini) is essentially a product of a human being's need to adapt himself at any time and in any circumstances to the challenges of his everyday environment — or so it should be. Unfortunately young individuals are so molded by the mentality of their parents, school, and culture that they take for granted the validity of principles they are taught and do not fully develop their ability to deal directly and spontaneously with their own immediate experiences. They may rebel against the pressures of their environment, but in so doing they are often as bound by their revolt as others are by their placid conformism.

♑
Capricorn

As the collective thinking-together of many minds engaged in social tasks becomes more complex and crystallized in general laws, agencies for the supervision of the applications and enforcement of these laws inevitably appear. Intuitions freeze into systems; group-solidarity engenders stable but restrictive social structures; common behavior glorifies itself in institutions. As the Night-Force reaches its greatest strength at the winter solstice — the beginning of Capricorn — society and its values dominate individual selfhood. The State tends to control the individual person, or the latter seeks power by identifying himself with the collective institution. He may appear to be a ruler, secure in his social office; yet his mind, feelings and conduct are often totally subservient to what this office demands of him. The tyrant is actually more a slave than his subjects; he is a slave to the image with which he has identified his whole being.

Nevertheless Capricorn brings to human beings the very great possibility of being the agent through whom the power of some vast super-individual Whole can be focused. Such a whole may be a social, communal or national whole; but it could also be the universal Whole. In Cancer man seeks rootedness and stability in a concrete soil, in a home; he strives after personal integration, from which he can derive personal power. Capricorn offers the possibility, latent in every seed, to be the focus for a whole species of life —

for mankind as a whole. The office controls the officiant; it also makes super-personal power available to him. It may bring him social immortality.

Aquarius

Every social position has some degree of power attached to it just as every person, because he is an integral bio-psychic organic whole, is able to use some kind of life-power. The possibility of using these two types of power — social and personal — is related to the two polar signs, Aquarius and Leo. Aquarius has recently been given very idealized and "Uranian" characteristics which are rather misleading. What it brings to man is simply the ability to use super-individual power: power to be used *in the name and for the sake of society,* or of mankind-as-a-whole.

In ancient astrology, Aquarius as well as Capricorn was ruled by Saturn. This rulership polarized that of Cancer and Leo by the two "Lights", Moon and Sun. In Cancer-Leo, man is and acts as an integrated, power-using individual person. In Capricorn-Aquarius, man is and acts as a *functioning agent of society.* He has a social position and he uses the power it bestows upon him. He uses it and enjoys the culture and social contacts which are related to his social position or prestige. What is at stake, I repeat, is no longer the vital energies of a physical organism through which Sun and Moon radiate life-power, but instead the power of social organization — and in some cases the power of the State, a Saturn-ian power. Aquarius reveals the possibility of bringing the social activities of a community to a cultural flowering — the possibilities of enjoying social or group togetherness as a kind of bonus on top of the fulfillment of merely personal needs. Thus many an "Aquarian" personality is very active in various kinds of groups, drawing social pleasure and fulfillment, from his participation in them as bees draw honey from flowers.

But work in many social positions and identification with institutional structures may not bring happiness and rewarding social contacts; they may lead to disappointment, conflicts with authorities, a refusal to conform and anti-social or revolutionary activities, but his purpose is to transform them and especially to comes in. Then the Aquarian may still participate in many group-activities, but his purpose is to transorm them and especially to change the quality of the use of energies released by interpersonal and social interplay. This is his utopian dream, and perhaps his life-work.

Pisces

The great possibility which Pisces offers to man is that of bringing a cycle of activity to an end pregnant with futurity; and this means *not* to accept death — or the end of any cycle of experience — as a final even after which nothing remains of what had been. Pisces therefore symbolizes the will to immortality and to transcendence — the will to gather the quintessence of what has been experienced into some kind of ''seed-form'' out of which more life may sooner or later emerge.

This basic characteristic of Pisces manifests in a variety of ways, but mainly as a deep yearning for whatever one may imagine to be beyond the familiar realm of body and sense experience. Thus, all kinds of devotional activities and attempts to obtain mystical realizations are favored, and also what today is called ''psychism''. Gross material experiences are left behind as worthless, and the consciousness is all open — often far too open and indiscriminately receptive — to whatever comes to it from unknown realms. Unfortunately the past does not die easily or swiftly. The open consciousness may find itself "invaded" by the karmic residua or ghosts of the unfulfilled past, whether it be the personal or even the collective-social past. Man must extract from Pisces the courage and strength to overcome and dismiss these ghosts, so that his consciousness may be a clean and revirginized soil to receive the true seeds of the future cycle.

Pisces can bring a great deal of drama to man because the most sensitive and critical moment of all existence is the moment in which the end of one cycle merges into the beginning of a new one. A person's attitude toward what has been conditions how he or she will meet the yet-to-be.

Mankind is living today, in a collective planetary sense, in a very critical period. Humanity's heavy past has to be transcended; yet it is still so attached to obsolete patterns that it seems very difficult for man to find the courage to dismiss all the ghostly presences and to face, unafraid, the transcending future. Flooded with memories of their "unfulfilled lives", and with a feeling of generalized guilt and therefore of imprecise fear before the Unknown, most human beings cling to what remains of seemingly secure traditions or try to escape into the formless and the unreal.

Astrology has been called (by Marc Jones, I believe) "the science of all beginnings". But it is as well the great art of bringing to a significant conclusion all experiences in which the potentiality of rebirth inheres. The study of the zodiac should help us to think of all our experiences as phases of an all-encompassing life-cycle. Every experience has had value; it has meaning in relation to the whole cycle. We must allow the memories of hesitancy, fear, traumas, and frustrations to disintegrate, and retain only the essential meanings. As Franklin D. Roosevelt once said: "The past is only prelude."

Every day can be a total rebeginning.

Zodiacal Signatures

♈ ARIES

The symbol of Aries is "germination." The soil filled with seed opens up to the descent of solar power, to the kiss of light. The one seed becomes the dualism of root and stem. And the stem itself branches out, that in the innermost place where Power is born the divine splendor of the fecundant Self may dwell — an inverted spark of the triune fire of the Creator whose countenance men adore and reflect in their puny procreations. The ideal of the "I am," symbolized in ancient Greece by the Doric column, freezes into the materiality of a personalized ego the mystic dance of union in which the spirit of Heaven rhythmically could touch the bent and expectant human soul. The "I" could be the mediator. Through "I" the universal forever seeks to bless the particular; in an antiphony of desire, the only-man aspires to be more-than-man in moments of appeased lucidity — rare as these may be.

Aries is passion of life. At the vernal equinox, death and birth meet in the symbolical Easter. In this meeting there is power, joy — incomprehension also. In Aries the nascent individual is lived by life; his mind may be wide open to the gift of the divine Host — the ever fecundant compassion of God, cyclically generating time to offer to the unfulfilled past a new opportunity to experience in organic selfhood the Harmony of the eternal Whole. But the passion of life is strong, unrelenting. Who will find in self the power to transcend its rhythmic urges, and ram with ensteeled mind-strength the walls life built to secure its redundance and proliferations?

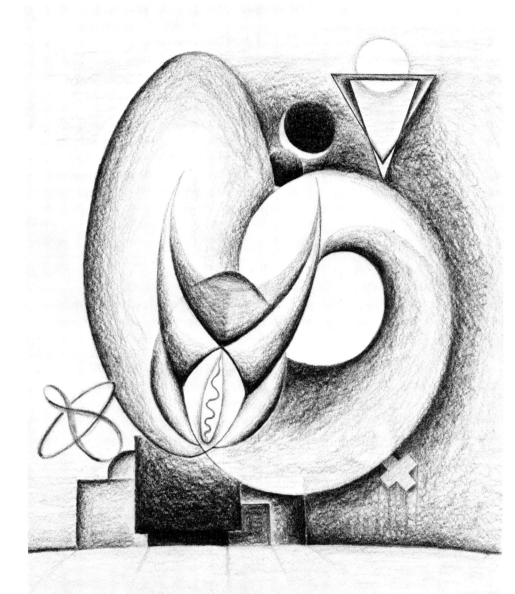

♉
TAURUS

Out of the cubic Stone of matter, differentiated into a myriad of crystalline structures, the flowing curves of living bodies take form. They open themselves to the power of light, carrying within its compassionate song the promise of individual existence. Venus, builder of magnetic fields that capture the electrical impulses of the creative spirit, brings to a focus the promise of wholeness, of fulfillment in love — a love that forever sings of the overcoming of pain and crucifixion.

At the mystic Hymen the power of tomorrow overcomes the inertia of yesterday. "Now" is the eternal battlefield where life's arrows pierce the resistance of matter. There Arjuna hears Krishna's exhortations, and the frightened ego is tuned up by the Supreme Will Transcending victory as well as defeat — always at peace with itself, ever serene, all-encompassing, pure beyond all concepts of defilement. There the Buddha renounces the illusory freedom of Nirvana to bind himself to Man in a conjugal rhythm of yearly overcoming and repolarization. There Life is celebrated in the minor mode of the sexual dance and the ecstasy of self-forgetting rises from the antiphony of polarized bodies. There bondage and freedom can be seen intertwined in the rope of becoming. Some may dance with it. Others it may strangle in death's illusory freedom. To be able to choose is Man's tragic glory.

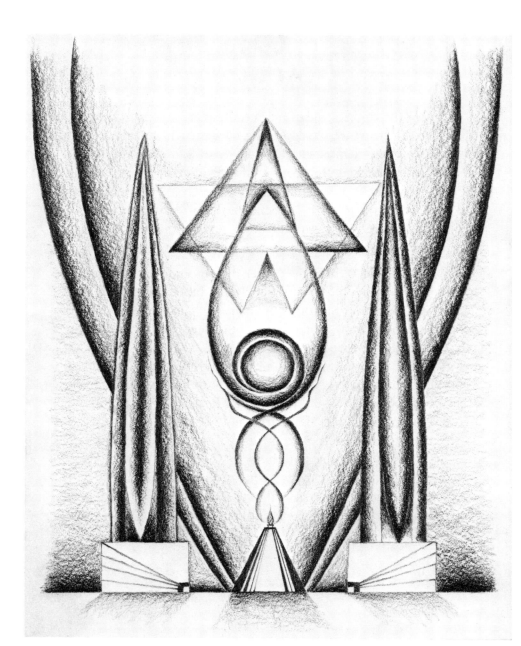

♊

GEMINI

When thinking of the Gemini symbol, most people visualize two pillars supporting a roof shutting from the sky a house of matter where the ego weaves its mind-patterns, as a spider its web. Our civilization is enamoured of walls and flat roofs, of pompous columns standing proudly to support only their own pride and self-glorification. But pillars may become flames; the space they define, an ardent field of cosmic vision, roofless and tonitruant. The exuberant, yet culture-bound mind at last may discover a galactic center from which to receive inexhaustible inspiration. The consciousness of Man may rise in spirallic ecstasy of transcendence from Earth-environment to ever vaster realms in which to participate in the birth of ever more inclusive ideas.

Yet, Man remains the definer and classifier of a reality whose pregnancy of self-transcendence he so often stubbornly refuses to recognize, lest the seemingly quake-proof structures of his normality should shatter under the irresistable impact of the solidarity of light. Fearsome and insecure, the ego-mind resists the impredictability of cosmic rhythms that, self-compensated though they be, always include for man the freedom of choice, and for God the great Play of unconstrained imaginings and humorous alternatives beyond human ratiocinations.

CANCER

Whatever our imagination pictures, sooner or later is bent into the curvatures of substantial reality. The winged mind sees itself reflected, and by that reflection emprisoned, in the massivity of matter. But out of the mass new forms appear. Buildings rise. In a passion of productivity, life seizes the mind's vision and makes of it a proliferation of even-repeated newborns. On our physical, all too physical planet, life reveals its power in an orgy of mass-productivity dwarfing Man's proud systems and assembly lines. Produce. More and more, always more — produce! Never cease until the sea is solid with fish, and the home a chaos of Children's babbling tongues. Produce! Build Babel towers to throw Man's material achievements at the face of uncomprehending stars! A day will come when depleted soil and polluted seas will rise in anger under resentful and sullen skies.

Through the crisis, Man's productivity and Nature's bounty will subside, exhausted, bewildered by their creations. Then matter may reveal its secrets and atoms sing galactic songs in choral harmony — never altered, yet never the same — always active, yet never unbalanced. In that day beyond the fatality of night, minds will bow — in adoration — before the revelation of a "most great Peace" whose dynamism is so intense, its rhythms so perfect, that to our bemused vision it seems to be an unending plateau of changelessness. This peace, it is Man's divine home.

♌
LEO

Every "I am" flamboyantly spreads its daimonic intensity in whorls of self-expression and self-glorification. It sees itself pictured in the eyes of beings it dynamized into hushed assent, if not servile worship — in the shapes its creative imagination summoned from the unformed and expectant substance of things that have mass and weight — in walls made alive with arabesques, and sounding boards pregnant with a myriad of potential tones.

Leo is the magician caught into the glamor of his magic, the leader resonating to the needs of his followers, the master who needs slaves to prove his mastery. Leo is the autocratic Sun, abolute ruler of his little cosmos, the **heliocosm.** Yet his "solar winds" cannot cross the boundaries of Saturn's orbit, for power-sheer, self-conscious power — is always limited by that which defines and measures its scope and gives it an individualized character.

But the Sun is also a star; and a day comes when this fact — recognized, accepted, welcome — transfigures heliocosmic space and all that lives within it. The rhythm of solar might fades out as the majestic gong of galactic being is heard within the chastized and assuaged heart. Everywhere individuals who once gloried in their names and forms humbly don the yellow robe of transcendent Brotherhood; and, shaded from the light, all eyes long for the darkness in whose silence all tones merge into the state of absolute repose — where there is nothing, where there is God.

VIRGO

Space is the Eternal Virgin, the absolute potentiality of numberless cosmic actualizations. Trillions of possible universes, each of which could sing its special song and reveal in its cyclic harvest a particular quality of existence brought to a state of perfection, are implied in its silence. They are born and die, protecting their specific solutions to the inexhaustible problems of existence in space-time fields of mental awareness, cosmic shells within which grow the multi-layered Pearl of Attainment, the harvest of meanings crystallized by pain and overcoming.

There must be shells to insulate Man's anguished yet multifarious search for significance, to guard vulnerable seekers from tangential escapes into meaninglessness. There must be sufferings, footstools to climb unto the many levels of peace. There must be failures to polarize the realizations of the Perfect Ones, and enable them to grow divine through long vigils of compassionate love.

This love, nurtured in Vestal purity, enfolds and heals tragic souls that, blinded by the light of perfection, could only respond to its sublimity by hating its source. But hate too is a cry of relatedness. The only unredeemable sin is indifference; for in indifference, man loses the power to move on — be it through love or hate — toward that which transcends all dualities, all existence, even the desire to be.

Freed from desire, the Traveler on the Path that leads to the Nowhere and the Nowhen begins to listen to the Voice of Silence. His hollowed out mind resonates to songs of Infinity. Because he no longer seeks, he becomes the goal.

LIBRA

In equilibrium there is peace; but what is peace if not the harmonized conflict of opposites? He who treads the Middle way the Buddha outlined becomes himself the battlefield. All gates are battlefields where past and future hurl themselves at the Now. At every threshold existence thunders forth: What of your Now?

Man may pursue his course, steady and undeviated by the claims of either extreme; or he may oscillate in to and fro dances, glorifying zigzags as Art and irresoluteness as fate-ordained compromise. But one does not compromise with the sublime Peace of buddhahood. Centered gyroscopically in undeviated motion, the Man of Peace ascends Gethsemane, as a lover the Beloved's expectancy. The song of Libra is a song of betrothal. In it every moment is the Beloved — to be caressed, to be fecundated in rhythmic union.

On this physical earth, groups and societies are built out of that union; new forms of communication, new symbols of oneness are born. Too often alas, the dream of unity finds itself rooted in the sandy, waterless soil of emotional repudiation of the past and social exclusivism; it crystallizes into collective egocentricity. Yet there is a realm where the fertile humus of an integral acceptance of all there is can sustain and make vivid the communion of Souls, companions in the "long March" to transcend freedom across mountains and deserts of loneliness. There is a realm that arches its all-encompassing peace over the last threshold. In front of it the Mystic Flower of nirvanic bliss is raised. How wonderful its perfume to the wearied soul! How enticing! Cull it, and all has been in vain. Ignore it, and all there has been, is and ever will become God — supreme Compassion, eternal Harmony.

SCORPIO

As the chill of autumnal skies is blown by passionate winds that tear from the trees the vestigial remains of estival splendor and made the soil shudder, the life-force recoils, hides within the roots. Could it mean defeat, or eventual rebirth? The issue must be met, consciously or unconsciously in this much abused sign of the zodiac. In consciousness there is hope, if not secure faith; in unconsciousness, heaviness and fear celebrate death as liberator from passion and sorrow. Jesus' cross stood upright, his head raised to the Father as he cried out, "My God, how hast thou glorified me! All is consummated;" but the Church, rooted in Peter's triple repudiation of Him who, only a few days before the Apostle had acclaimed as the Messiah, not only has relived for centuries the inverted cross of the Repudiator's martyrdom; it turned Jesus' words upside down. Man forgets; but God cannot, for in God's mind there is no past. Everything is now; Autumn is spring, death is birth.

When Mars' passion becomes conscious it flings itself, eagle-like, to the source of life and light; or else, frightened, it collapses into meaninglessness and ravenous hunger for the products of death. The sun is so low in late autumn that the eagle may tear from it sparks of divinity; but will the wings collapse burnt by the fire, or will they become translucent poems chanted to the rhythm of light? Will they stir men that are but human into seekers of the star that is their apocalyptic self? Scorpio is the eternal question tearing at the core of all roots under autumnal skies. Will it be death; will it be rebirth?

SAGITTARIUS

Sagittarius is the Moment made into an arrow shot at tomorrow's heart. It is the Particular burning with the yearning for the Universal — Man bending his animal nature upward to see God face to face, as a friend meets a friend. It is Man turning his ever-repeated cross into a jet-engine to raise himself starward with the flaming power of his repudiation of earthly roots.

Alas, the gravitational pull of the soil — the unconscious taken-for-granted, cohesive energy of family, culture and society — makes most human beings translate their starward longings into the more acceptable prose of social fellowship and institutionalized religion. The centrifugal passion of conquerors of space bends comfortably; it changes into social ambulations along horizontal golf courses, and alchemical retorts are museum pieces exchanged for club lounging chairs. Good old Jupiter forgets his lightning-bolts when faced with a gourmet dinner; even his Leda turns from beloved into a swan to be prepared as exotic roast for delighted guests.

When will the Crusade for righteousness that dreamt of human beings unite in a galaxy of companionate minds and dedicated souls become free of power politics and business greed, and restored to its transcendent status? When will the flaming thrusts of human minds burn benumbing factories of knowledge and liberate men, women, children for great spiritward adventures? When will Godmen be born?

♑

CAPRICORN

Meditation on power. The human earth, level after level rises to Himalayan intensity. A divine Presence overshadows the meditator, as the garnet sun sinks into the abyss. It merges with the quest. It is yogic power taking form as the embodied ideal, the vision made substance. Capricorn is a song of incarnation. God descends into man. The Universal acquires "form and name" according to the longing of particular beings seeking to insure the permanency of ideals. In China, the Emperor stood as Mediator between the celestial order and the inborn chaos of human nature — the central point of reference for all social drives. In India, the image of the Divine King, the **Chakravartin,** took form, both servant and ruler. Around him, the wheel of existence inexorably whirled. In the Christian world, Christ is King, but not of "this" world. His is the Kingdom of Heaven — from which divine Grace flows, blessing the pure in heart, whose translucent ego glows with compassionate power and effulgent love.

In Capricorn, right proclaims and demonstrates its might. What puny men oppose as moral contrast, the great Capricornians unify in the might of right, the power of Truth. They embody Truth, as they dispense justice as agents of the Law before which gods and men are but ripples on the surface of the infinite Ocean of uncontainable Space and inexhaustible possibilities. And teh world is at peace, for everything is what it is, nothing but what it is. Freedom is necessity; the Golden Age, and Eternal Now.

AQUARIUS

Power of the lightning! Matter summons anti-matter to celebrate nuptials of Fire; and in their self-annihilating embrace a new star is born, a chant of new possibility. The electric Waters of Space pour with Uranian glee upon those who, pillars of assimilating and rejoicing strength, stand as lightning rods to convey to the yet-unborn the mantram of galactic being. The Individual towers over the slow breathing masses in parturition of tomorrows. Will their inchoateness accept the flowing words of the transpersonal Heroes through whom God speaks of the future? Alas, too often tomorrow but mirrors exhausted yesterdays. The hero's voice is lost in the multitude of undifferentiated moans oozing out from the snow and mud of Karmic avalanches.

Power of the lightning! Sheets of fire down upon the dedicated Soul. A fervor of self-renewing invades the titubating mind, in ecstasy of severance from the past. Circles become spirals. The lost equilibrium surf-boards from crest to crest. Will the traveler on the waves of time flouder upon sandy shores, crash upon ragged rocks, or gloriously grow wings to meet the Yet-unknown on the mountain peaks where a new god awaits?

Alas, how few the meetings on Sinais of human experience! Aquarian babbling and socializing hide the impotency of effective rebirth. When will silence offer its golden space as womb for unclassified tomorrows?

PISCES

Out of the inexhaustible Ocean of potentiality, a Grail can always emerge to receive the new blood of an ever reborn Christ. In the magic instant — concentrate of silence — at which the wave of the past shyly draws away from the kiss of tomorrow, the unexpected may take birth; a new dream may redden the face of human hope. for a moment that is eternity the breath of yesterday hesitates. A new flow of **prana** fills the distended lungs. The consciousness reels, uncrtain of its roots, so beautiful is the dream of unconceived tomorrows — but alas, so distant, so vast, incomprehensibly vast the curve of time, so bare the horizon floating in mists of unconsciousness!

There are some who seize the sword Alexander carried from victory to victory to cut the Gordian Knot — the entanglements of time and cycles, of frustration and self-loss in pointless activity and passionate illusions — but many are the confused and the deluded. The Grail metamorphoses into beer cans; the divine Presence into phantoms of an unlived life. Yet every end can be rebeginning. Every **"Consummatum est"** can be a song of imminent Resurrection. At every corner of time, Easter can be met, and fragrant lilies soothe the breath so long nauseated by the stench of cities and decaying egos. Pisces is a song of hope, a paean of translucent faith. It cries out for light; and light will respond, if the cry modulates into song, and the widowed mind opens its deepest abysses to the rebirth of love.

12 Qualities Required for the Spiritual Life

Twelve Qualities Required for the Spiritual Life and Their Zodiacal Correspondences

by Dane Rudhyar

When many people think of living a spiritual life, especially if they are young and eager, their imagination often pictures unusual modes of existence, long periods of meditation, perhaps ascetic practices or spectacular tests and achievements, and not infrequently, travel to India in search of a guru or mysterious Brotherhoods. In earlier periods, the spiritual life was in most cases associated with a complete dedication to some religious institution. Today the identification of "spiritual" with "religious" is no longer taken for granted. Spirituality need not be equated with devotion to a system of religious beliefs; it should not be characterized by the *beliefs* of a person but by the *quality* of his or her actions, feelings and mental processes.

Spirituality is demonstrated at the three levels of behavior, feeling-responses and thinking. It is essentially a matter of motivation and of the way one actually approaches everyday experiences and meetings with other people. It refers to a quality of being, from which what one may call "virtues" are spontaneously derived. The individual may, and indeed should, spontaneously strive to embody these virtues in acts, feelings and thoughts. However, he or she should not do so tensely and with the kind of ego-posture expressing itself in a kind of "I'll show you, Lord!"

61

attitude. The striving should be conscious, steady, diligent and firm, yet without strain, and even less morbidity, for strain produces psychic toxins which can be as detrimental as a toxic condition of the physical body after an over-rigorous and inflexible schedule of muscular work.

Spiritual living does not require asceticism, except in the relatively rare instances in which an individual is inwardly ready to accept such a rigorous form of existence. The same is true of long, sustained meditations. Many young and not-so-young persons today are attracted to practices devised by such Oriental schools of spiritual development as Hindu Yoga or Japanese Zen. But this eagerly desired "spiritual development" is not always really spiritual, at least not in the sense which is most relevant to our Western mentality. It may well produce unusual and inspiring "experiences", but the questions arise: what is the value of these experiences? Can they be truly assimilated? What really occurs *after* the experience, when the consciousness that has been amazed and transported by it returns to our everyday life? How deep may be the shadow which the unredeemed ego often casts upon the briefly illumined consciousness?

At least for us, men and women who have to pursue our lives in the so often intellectually and emotionally polluted atmosphere of this American society, spirituality should rather imply a deeply felt and unconditional practice of what so many people may call "homely" virtues. But if these virtues are unsentimentally understood without reference to old stereotyped descriptions, their meanings can reach to the deepest levels of human existence. If they appear homely and unspectacular, this is because our conventional morality and religious doctrines have failed to realize that they belong to the warp and woof of all existence, that they have the most "cosmic" overtones. In order to present these virtues in their most universal and essential meanings, I shall now relate them to the signs of the zodiac. What by so doing I am attempting to show is how *twelve qualities* of living, each related to a zodiacal sign, can be seen to be essential to a truly spiritual life.

Every birth-chart includes all twelve signs of the zodiac. Each sign contributes some essential factor to the character and personality of a newborn. In any particular chart, some signs are emphasized by the presence of planets, or by the fact of their appearing at the four Angles of the chart. As a result, the astrologer can establish the basic "formula" characterizing an individual's personality. I have taught for many years that a person's birth-chart thus constitutes a "message" from the universe; it is a *set of instructions* given to him or her at birth by the Sky. It is the "celestial Name" of the individual — a Name more fundamentally valid and true than the name inherited from the parents and their culture and religion.

This Name therefore gives us more significant clues concerning the relative importance of certain virtues in our attempts to live in terms of spiritual values. I should note, however, that in any particular birth-chart, the connections between zodiacal signs emphasized by planets or Angles and the "qualities of living" I shall relate to the signs are not to be taken too literally. Nevertheless, they can most often point to certain areas of our existence in which the practice of the related qualities may prove worthwhile, strenghening and illumining.

Twelve Zodiacal Qualities of Spiritual Living

Courage

As I see it, this is as necessary a foundation for spiritual living as Aries and all it represents on this earth is basic in any wholesome (or "holistic") grasp of what the zodiac represents wherever there is life and growth. The spiritual life is practically never an easy life, at least not in our present-day society. It fundamentally implies an *emergence* from usually quite binding and possessive psychic and social matrices: family, culture, religion, tradition, way of life. Such an emergence and spiritual life built upon its foundation requires struggle, and very often involves tense conflicts. Confrontations may be strenuous. They call for courage, unrelenting courage; and behind courage stands WILL. Indeed, will stands behind all that pertains to the spiritual life, just as the Sun stands behind all zodiacal signs which constitute twelve fundamental aspects of the one solar energy. The will to be born anew of the spirit, by the power of spirit and for the spiritual purpose of one's existence is what energizes all truly spiritual efforts.

The spiritual life is not a life emotionally devoted to some special form of spiritual revelation; that kind of life should rather be called "religious." The spiritual life is life lived *from* the spirit, *by* the spirit, *for* the spirit. It implies a basic surrender of the ego-will to the "solar" Will. The individual person becomes, and irrevocably accepts to become, an "agent" of the spirit. Such an acceptance must be conscious, even if it surges from a depth of being which transcends everyday consciousness. At the very least the

64

consciousness must put its stamp upon the decision; and this demands courage — a lucid kind of courage if the basic decision is to become truly and effectively implemented by a multitude of small, everyday choices. Likewise, through all signs of the zodiac, especially the first six, the energy mobilized in Aries remains the fundamental factor. Where it is lacking, the activities characterizing every zodiacal sign can only be superficial. The whole person is like a bell from which but a hollow sound can be produced.

Non-Possessiveness

Where there is possessiveness and clinging to loved ones out of insecurity, fear or pride, there can be no spiritual living. The desire to possess whatever or whomever has brought us pleasure or happiness, ease and the fulfillment of a personal need is most natural; but the spiritual life is not a life of subservience to nature and its instinctual, bio-psychic wants. It is a life of transcendence. Natural impulses which are always at root compulsive and mostly unconscious have to be transcended.

This is the great issue which separates the spiritual life from the type of existence which modern psychology tends to idealize, although such an idealization is valid as a transitional feature. American men and women have to be *de-conditioned* so that they may forget their varied complexes and the rigidity of feelings and body-responses imposed upon them by the Puritan tradition and the pompous hypocrisy of Victorian age morality. In spite of the permissiveness of modern education, the very persons who claim to be "free" are so often bound by subtle, or not so subtle, forms of possessiveness and fear — jealousy being but another form of fear.

The zodiacal sign Taurus is traditionally thought to be a possessive sign, but its possessiveness arises from its concentration upon *productivity.* In order to produce a rich harvest, limits have to be set to the field in which natural process have to operate efficiently. Ownership is part of the limiting process. There must be a concentration of efforts, a focusing will to keep away all interfering activities. But productivity at a higher level also requires an openness to fecundating external influences — openness to the whole universe.

Possession, however, need not mean *binding attachment.* There is a level at which the Taurean capacity to produce fruits can operate, not in an "indefinite," but rather in a multi-defined or universally operative manner. One can thus transcend the "This is *mine*" mentality. The demand for an exclusive sense of possession is usually based on fear — which means on *the inability to possess oneself*. It is rather easy not to be possessive of material goods when one lives in a convent or a group-situation where total sharing of objects being used is the rule. But such situations, valid as they undoubtedly can be at the transitional stage of deconditioning, often drive possessiveness and fear into deeper and mostly unconscious or un-acknowledged levels. In true spiritual living these illusions are discarded. The individual can stand and act unpossessively in the very midst of possessions. One may experience "poverty" in conditions of affluence. All that matters, or should matter, is that whatever is *necessary* for the activity at hand should be available. Whether one owns it is irrelevant, provided one can make use of it for the achievement of a purpose which is essentially super-personal — super-personal because the spiritual individual fully accepts being simply the agent for the fulfillment of this purpose.

Intellectual Honesty

Many people might not see at first how the words "intellectual" and "honesty" can be linked, and even less what role they can play in a spiritual life. The reason for this is twofold: We mainly relate honesty to personal behavior and primarily to the handling of money or of matters of social value; and we have been repeatedly told that spirituality has nothing to do with the intellect, that it belongs to a different level of existence entirely.

Spirit nevertheless can and does operate at *any* level of human existence. It can pervade and transfigure all mental processes. It can transmute all emotional expressions. The word, honesty likewise defines a quality of being which should be demonstrated at all levels. There is such a thing as "emotional honesty," and beyond it stands what I call here intellectual honesty — a quality which may be significantly related to the zodiacal sign Gemini.

The opposite of honesy is deceit. An individual can deceive others, either unwillingly or deliberately. This can happen in terms of feelings, and even more perhaps in connection with mental processes. One of the great dangers in any endeavor to live a spiritual life is self-deception. On one hand, one can deceive oneself concerning the motives of these endeavors. On another, one can avoid critically and objectively investigating the life and claims of whoever one accepts as one's "teachers" or exemplars, because an objective and unglamorized approach could be energy-consuming or even painful.

The sign Gemini has much to do with the intellect, that is, with the ability to relate various experiences and concepts to one another, then to interpret, generalize and classify them. These intellectual operations are normally performed by the mind according to certain cultural norms or rational standards. Yet they are not inevitably so performed. People often come to believe intellectually what they emotionally *want* to believe. The Gemini mind is tricky and elusive. It tends to run hither and thither, swayed by non-mental states of feelings, desires or moods. Thus self-deceit is a constant danger.

To be intellectually honest is to refuse to allow factors which are not intellectually sound, and even more which are the results of emotional wants, to interfere with one's thinking. It is to recognize for what they are and what they produce the factors of pride, fear, and of the immature longing for props to support one's dim understanding of transcendent facts and values. Without intellectual honesty the finest endeavors may miscarry. Glamor is the enemy — even if it is most often needed at the beginning of the spiritual quest to "fascinate" us into taking steps which arouse otherwise paralyzing instinctual or emotional fears. Needed as they may be at first, glamor and deceit must be overcome as soon as possible, or else spirituality turns into "psychism."

Sensitivity

This word is used here in its most positive aspect, but it can be unfortunately applied to biological and psychological conditions which are not relevant to spiritual living. A person can be not only abnormally, but morbidly sensitive to all kinds of impressions and suggestions. The spiritual life does not accept passivity to external impacts or internal pressures as a valuable factor. Yet positiveness does *not* mean that senses, feelings, mind and intuition should be "set" in any rigid manner. One can be totally open to the universe, yet positive in one's attitude toward what comes into the field of one's consciousness.

The field of one's consciousness is, in a sense, one's "home" — thus the elation to Cancer. But it should not be a jealously guarded field, and much less a fortified castle. There should be a constant commerce of values between the inner and outer worlds — and no rigidly protective tariff. If an individual has not the sensitivity needed to vibrate freely under the impact of a great variety of experiences, and to resonate to vibrations reaching him or her from higher and subtler realms of existence and consciousness, then such a person's spiritual living is poor indeed, and his or her progress is very slow.

Man's greatest asset along the tortuous path of planetary evolution in the biosphere has been his unusual sensitivity, his awareness of subtle clues and half-hidden or remote possibilities. Sense-awareness, feeling-awareness, mental awareness and intuition combine to provide man with a very delicate type of sensitivity. This sensitivity must not be unsteady and overwhelm the core of consciousness. Courage is required in order not to fear it. As the mind attempts to interpret the messages it receives and to deduce from them — without allowing itself to be self-deceived — guiding lines in the pursuit of an ever-higher, more encompassing goal, the quality of non-possessiveness is also necessary; for in order to be truly open and sensitive, one has to be positive and secure, yet non-attached to past experiences.

70

Simplicity

One of the deepest and often well-camouflaged pitfalls encountered in the spiritual life is a tendency for *self-dramatization* and, at a further stage of involvement, self-glorification. It may start with the feeling that one is quite "special," or that the group one belongs to is blessed with a unique and direct connection with some Master, or even with God. The next step is a deliberate or unconscious attempt to give to what may be rather ordinary or unspectacular happenings an extraordinary significance — a dramatic significance which places one's action in an especially exalting light. This sooner or later feeds a growing sense of pride and spiritual achievement.

An individual may indeed have made notable progress in his or her development. One may witness in oneself the emergence of relatively unusual and fascinating new powers or faculties (for instance, clairvoyance, telepathic communication, etc.). These experiences may well be impressive; but unfortunately what they also impress is the ego with its own special importance. Moreover, such experiences can be used to impress others with the importance of the experience — or rather, of his or her ego. Even suffering and tragedy — or "attacks" by dark Forces — can become instruments for self-dramatization.

The Leo type of temperament is particularly apt to indulge in this kind of feeling and to dramatize itself, but we all have something of such a tendency in us. For this reason, the Church has always demanded humility and obedience of all who sought to dedicate themselves to spiritual transformation. The proud ego had to humble itself in every possible manner, and to give up any sense of being "special" and extraordinary, favored by God — even if this meant favored by spectacular tragedies or opportunities to perform deeds which seemed divinely inspired.

Today in our ego-exalting society, the word humility does not have a very attractive appeal. I have therefore used the term simplicity, which has a broader application and in every instance goes to the root of the matter. Simplicity is the antidote for self-dramatization. Complexity and the urge for psychological self-glamorization almost always lead to some form of pride. This pride may be camouflaged through the use of noble gestures, even gestures of self-humiliation. The truly spiritual person is not only humble; his acts are direct and simple. He is simply and purely what he is. Others may place all kinds of mysterious or wondrous interpretations upon his simple actions; but the spiritual person makes no claim. He lets his works speak for themselves, as he "walks on" toward an ever fuller actualization of his innate potential of being.

Discrimination

The qualities mentioned so far have a basically subjective character. They refer to the will, the feelings, the mental development and the way the individual allows his or her energies to respond to and flow outward into the surroundings. As a result of this complex personal activity, the individual is faced with the necessity of considering alternatives, of making choices and decisions. In order to be spiritually significant these require discrimination.

It is unfortunate that today the word discimination is popularly used in terms of discimination *against* a person or class of persons. True discrimination operates *between* alternatives — right and wrong, good and better, etc. Discrimination is needed at the mental, emotional, biological and social-cultural levels so that situations which a person meets can be objectively analyzed and evaluated in order to be meaningfully acted upon.

A clear mind and glamor-free sense of values are essential. However, most everything depends on the *standards* of intellectual honesty and of value which consciously or not, the individual accepts. Underlying one's thinking must be some basic principles or beliefs to which the individual refers, even if he cannot precisely and clearly explain, to himself as well as to others, why he passes his intellectual, moral or feeling judgments.

The zodiacal sign Virgo has been called the sign of discipleship because to become the disciple of a great Teacher or to serve a Cause implies a determination to find a reliable foundation upon which a sound sense of discrimination can be built. One's discriminations may seem sound to the disciple and not to other persons, but this does not essentially matter. What matters, at the level of the spiritual life, is that the individual no longer takes for granted and unquestioningly accepts a traditional, inherited basis for discrimination, but that he makes a deliberate effort to discover what *to him as an individual* is true or false, valid or invalid.

Equanimity in Love

There is a tendency, particulary among idealistic young people to equate spirituality and love. Love is the light that illumines "the Path" which the individual who has consecrated his or her life to the highest value treads. It is a way filled with obstacles and deceiving shapes, fascinating half-truths and ideals camouflaging ego-wants. Without the light of love, the "walking on" would indeed be dreary and might lead to abysses of darkness; but love does not do the walking. Will and courage are the first requisites. They lead, and later on wisdom becomes the guide, as light takes on the form of one who has gone before over the path and, out of love and compassion, waits for the struggling aspirant rather than take the final step to blissful transcendence.

Yet all loves are not light. How many follies and crimes have been perpetrated in the name of love! How binding, possessive and disturbing or devastating a lover can be! This is why I speak here of a rate virtue, "equanimity in love" — love which is deeply peaceful, serene, which requires no passionate responses, which remains love even if seeming indifference or neglect is the response, which is truly a gift, a sharing of what one *is* far more than what one *has*.

"Equanimity" implies inner peace and security. The individual is truly equal to all occasions, quietly but reliably available when needed. The possible fruits of the love are placed on the altar of one's dedication to the highest value — call it God if you wish — there to be blessed, or burned as useless material, or as incense, to add a rich, warm fragrance to the so often sordid atmosphere of man's daily existence. This love *is*. One does not have to grow into it, to work at it. It is the inner radiance of one's own being, ready to flow into whoever can *resonate* to its vibrations and commune in its peace. It is egoless and unaffected by storms.

A great dream, indeed this is; yet we can try to incorporate it into our total being. As we do so, we live up to the highest potential of the equinoctial sign Libra.

74

Non-Competitive Efficiency

A person seeking to lead a spiritual life often fails to realize that he (or she) has to display "efficiency" in his pursuits, if he is to reach his high goal. Such a person should be able to redirect or repolarize and transform the biological and psychological energies of his human nature, and he should be efficient in so doing; otherwise he will not stand the pressure of opposing forces — the shadow side of his personality. He will either fall by the wayside, disocurged by half-successes and only too ready to give up his quest, or he may become fascinated by someone or some group which promises wonderful results at the cost of only small efforts and thanks to some special outside help.

The spiritual life is a very demanding kind of life. There are no easy shortcuts. The will and the mind must be clearly focused upon anything being attempted; yet while efficiency in action and thought has to be shown, one should not passionately seek results. Results do not matter as much as the quality of the act or the thought. One should not be attached to the fruits of the action; yet one must see that whatever is done is done efficiently, precisely and on time.

This is not what we usually relate to the mystical way, but such a way is, alas, so often misrepresented and misunderstood. It too is a hard way, and above all a paradoxical way. It asks of one utter dedication to a goal, the achievement of which does not matter, because, in a sense, there is no "goal," but only a process of unfoldment of what is and always has been there *potentially*. It asks moreover that all forms of ambition be relinquished — and "spiritual" ambition may be the most dangerous, withal most subtle, kind of ambition. Ambition must not be the motive for being efficient. There should be no feeling whatsoever of competition in one's endeavors, especially if one is part of a group of seekers or disciples. It does not matter if one appears to be first or last, for the competitive spirit is a form of violence, and there can be no violence in the soul of the true disciple on the spiritual Path.

The zodiacal sign Scorpio tends to be associated with violence and competition, because the Scorpio type of person is often too emotionally and personally involved in making of human relationships what to him or her is a "success." Such a person becomes so intensely involved in experiencing love, friendship, sharing, and activity in common that he might forget in the experience his isolation or alienation — which essentially means his basic insecurity.

The spiritual person does not cling to his actions or the results of his actions. He does whatever is necessary for him to do as effectually and thoroughly as possible. He does it for "God," for the Spirit within him, regardless of how the action will affect his social or spiritual status. He does it unhurriedly, noncompetitively, without any motive except the fulfillment of his destiny, i.e. of his place and function in the universe.

Creative Visualization

One of the fundamental concepts in occultism, and even in modern New Thought, is that man can only become what he is able consciously to imagine, or more precisely to "image forth." This is the reason why Avatars, divine Manifestations or spiritual Teachers have to appear among the masses of men when the time for a basic *mutation,* or radical transformation of the implications of human existence, has struck on the vast clock of evolution. Such Personages embody the main characteristics of the "new step" which mankind, or a section of mankind, has now to take. They are Exemplars. They stimulate, mobilize or fascinate human beings into doing what the latter would otherwise be unwilling and too inert to do. Looking at these Exemplars, human beings who have felt within themselves a vague yet poignant sense of discontent and restlessness *see* clearly realized in the life of the Exemplar the ideal power or virtue for which they more or less unconsciously longed.

Every person on the spiritual Path must, in a sense, be his or her own avatar. One has to embody in concrete forms and deeds the ideal that is *potentially* one's own being. In order to embody it, the individual must visualize it clearly. He must mobilize himself; he must create himself. The spiritual life is always the creation of him who lives it; and he lives it because first of all he has imagined it. He has creatively visualized what he *knew* deep in his heart to be his butterfly-self. He has done so while still in the chrysalis state, the Dark Night of the Soul.

This is the Great Work of the true alchemist at the level of mind. But this visualizing mind is not what we today usually call mind. It is mind *plus* will, *plus* faith and vibrant openness to ever-new possibilities — the Sagittarian "Higher Mind". It has been said of the conservative person that he is one who refuses to believe that anything can ever happen for the first time. To the creative imagination of a mind infused with spirit, every moment is a first time. Such an individual lives in a passion of creative discovery, in an ever-repeated act of rebirth.

Self-Reliance

The spiritual kind of self-reliance is based upon an inner realization that one is forever able to create oneself anew to meet life's challenges and opportunities. It has little to do with the egocentric and ambitious pride of the individual whose physical vitality and intellectual cunning assure him of a successful type of one-upmanship in social encounters. Spiritual self-reliance does not mean blatant or ruthless ego-assertion. It is rather a quiet but steady sense of ineradicable trust in the power of the spirit within to work toward what ultimately is cosmic or divine "rightness," whatever superficial or temporary weaknesses or disappointments may arise. It is a deep incontrovertible feeling that God's will — or the vast movement of planetary and human evolution — will be fulfilled when the proper season comes. It is the realization within the seed covered by wintry snow of the Capricorn season that spring must come; and it is an utter reliance upon the validity of such a realization.

The important factor in this kind of spiritual self-reliance is an unwillingness *to depend* on intermediaries between oneself and the Divine. One certainly can and should readily and gratefully accept the help of others in limited and well-defined circumstances, and particularly during crises of growth; but one should not allow one's emotions — fear or despondency — to cling to such help. Assistance should rather be considered an act of Providence, a focusing of divine love and compassion operating *through* another person much more than *from* this person. The intermediary is not the essential factor; the source of the downflow of "grace" is what alone counts, what alone one should depend upon.

The tragedy of the (strictly speaking) "religious" life is that it fosters a dependence upon the intermediary; and the present upheaval in the Roman Catholic world is, in its deepest meaning, a spiritual revolt against the feeling that one *must* depend upon intermediaries in order to reach God or even to be "saved". Indeed all religious institutions are to some extent experiencing such an upheaval; and the same is true in a different context of political or social institutions. Such is the great revolution underneath many superficial revolts — often premature, always emotional and dependent upon some form of violence. The truly self-reliant man — the highest Capricorn type of person — is at peace with himself and the universe, even as he struggles against the inertia of institutionalized dependence on all types of "middle men."

A Sense of Humor

Strange as it may seem to many people, a sense of humor is quite indispensable to a successful pursuit of a spiritual life. No individual can be truly spiritual who, at times, is not able to laugh at himself, and to smile at the theatrical gestures and claims of others. *Taking oneself too seriously* is one of the most common and insidious dangers a person meets on the spiritual Path. A sense of proportion, and the realization of how small a role one may play in the cosmic ritual of world-existence, needs to be cultivated, if one's idealistic and "so-well-intentioned" service to a social or spiritual community is not to backfire and throw most of its warmth upon an ego becoming increasingly full of its own importance.

Today we readily tend to glorify out of all proportion anything related to the zodiacal sign Aquarius — including the so eagerly expected Aquarian Age itself. This may be unfortunate, at least from a spiritual point of view, for it can lead to what Carl Jung called "self-inflation" and to extravagant hopes concerning what the "New Age" may bring, especially during its first centuries. It is one thing to deliberately and perhaps emotionally dedicate oneself to "world service", and another to glamorize one's ability to carry on such a dedication in everyday pursuits without faltering. The one antidote against self-inflation is a sense of humor.

One should work and strive as if that only mattered; but while doing it one ought to keep a mirror handy and often look sideways at how funny a face the mirror reflects — sideways, not full face, for if you look at yourself full face you will naturally take an unduly serene or over-dramatic pose. The greatest danger in being surrounded by eager and devoted disciples is that looking into their eyes, the teacher sees himself glorified. Disciples too should learn compassionately to smile at their teacher's claims or postures, so that he may be helped not to take himself too seriously.

Faith in the Future

Such a faith is what the Pisces type of person needs in order to overcome the insidious pressures of the "ghosts" of his or her race's past. Such a person should also be careful not to dwell constantly in the "psychic realm" filled with such astral presences or emotional memories, or within the realm where the great institutions and cultural-religious traditions of past centuries still pursue their now often obsolescent existence. The past is to be known, evaluated, appreciated for what in it was vitalizing and promising of futurity. One shoud not *feel* in terms of the past, or allow oneself to be conditioned by memories of either happiness and success, or of failure, guilt and perhaps tragedy.

The past most often towers, in cantilever fashion, over the present. It throws its shadow upon the future, which it seeks to mould in its own image, or at times in terms of the reverse aspect of this image. Today we hear over and over again that we must live in the present, in the Now. But there is a basic naivety in such statement. Life is a dynamic process, and what we awkwardly call "the present" is simply *the movement* from past to future.

This movement is conditioned by what has happened before — by our language, our culture, our individual formation in childhood and what society expects of us according to its repetitive patterns. If we are not to become a duplication of these patterns we need to have a vibrant, creative faith in the future — a future that *could* be different from the past, because more evolved, more fulfilling.

Pisces is the end of a cycle, but also the prelude to a new one. As Franklin D. Roosevelt said: "The past is only prelude." The seed too is also a prelude to the future vegetation. Within the "seed man" the vision of the new culture glows, vivid and potent. It alone can redeem the past and give it constructive significance.

The Twelve Qualities in Relation to Your Birth-Chart

The twelve qualities or virtues described in the foregoing can be referred to a person's birth-chart because of their relationship to the signs of the zodiac. The most significant way of doing this is to consider the signs which are found at the four Angles of the chart — and secondarily, at the cusps of the various Houses. As I see it, the natal Houses (calculated for the exact time of the first breath) represent twelve basic categories of experiences which every individual has to meet as he or she lives and unfolds the innate potentialities of his or her nature. The zodiacal sign at the cusp of a House gives us a clue as to the type of quality one *should* stress as one deals with the kind of experience to which this House refers. The four angular Houses — whose cusps are the Ascendant, the astrological Nadir, the Descendant and the Zenith — are by far the most important, for they deal with the four categories of experiences which are basic in structuring the development of the personality.*

If for instance we consider a birth-chart with a Sagittarius Ascendant, we would deduce from this fact that the person *should* find the development of "creative visualization" (or imagination) essential, if he is to discover his true individuality — the spiritual "tone" of his unique selfhood and destiny. If I say "should," it is because, according to the approach to astrology I have been formulating and promoting for many years, astrology is far more valuable in revealing to us the basic quality and purpose which life, God of the universe wants us to fulfill than in indicating what can only be a probability — never a certainty — of precise events yet to come.

*For a thorough discussion of what the natal Houses of a birth-chart represent, the interested reader is referred to my book *The Astrological Houses: The Spectrum of Individual Experience* (Doubleday Co., N.Y.: 1972).

The person with a Sagittarius Ascendant inevitably has a Gemini Descendant; thus, the value for him to develop "intellectual honesty" in interpersonal relationship, i.e., in all forms of partnership or association. If Libra is at the Midheaven, what is indicated is the importance of demonstrating "equanimity in love" in his public role or professional activities. This of course has to be interpreted very broadly, and in such an analysis one must hold in mind that these twelve qualities should be applied mainly to persons who, in some degree, are seeking to live according to a vision and purpose. At the fourth House cusp Aries would then be found, showing that "courage" is necessary in dealing with one's feeling-nature, with parents and home, and with all that refers to the very roots of the personality.

When a zodiacal sign is emphasized by the presence of several planets, problems or issues referring to the spiritual quality related to this sign are likely to arise. In the chart of President F.D. Roosevelt, four planets (Saturn, Neptune, Jupiter and Pluto) are in Taurus. The character-factor of "non-possessiveness" is seen to bring a very basic, heavy confrontation. Since F.D.R. reached the Presidency at a time of financial crisis, he had to face great issues dealing with "possessiveness" in the nation — i.e. with men clinging to privileges and wealth, and in general with the entire question of the value of the "profit system". His three planets in Aquarius also stressed the need for a healthy "sense of humor", and his rising Uranus in Virgo revealed the need for "discrimination" in revolutionary circumstances. The value of objectively assessing the relative value of alternatives at such a critical time was therefore emphasized.

In the chart of the English ex-Prime Minister, Harold Wilson, the Cancer Ascendant reveals a need for personal "sensitivity"; but the Ascendant is surrounded by Pluto and Saturn, which probably have created problems and blockages in the development of this quality. Yet one cannot judge how the spiritual life of such a public figure may have developed, or may develop in later years. Dr. Roberto Assagioli, founder of the Psychosynthesis movement and a true spiritual leader, also had Cancer rising; but Pisces was at the Midheaven with the Sun and Mercury near this zenith point. Under great difficulties, especially during World War II, he demonstrated a vibrant "faith in the future"; and his Virgo Nadir (with Moon close by in opposition to the Sun) stresses the value of "discrimination."*

Space does not permit more examples, and such an approach to a birth-chart does not lend itself well to the study of public personages. It deals with the most intimate factors in the personality, and is mostly significant to individuals who aspire to develop the full spiritual potentialities of their innate nature.

---

*These charts can be found in my book *Person-Centered Astrology* (ASI Publishers, 1980).

Astrological Themes
for Meditation

On Meditation

In this period of deep psychological and ideological up-heavals, two words have gained an unusual amount of prom-inence; meditation and astrology. These two words polarize or complement each other in an interesting way.

In the minds of most people meditation implies some kind of inward process leading the consciousness towards its greater depths and its essential foundation in pure, abstract being. On the other hand, according to the popular understanding of its nature, astrology is thought to provide a knowledge of forces acting upon every aspect of a person's or a nation's life and determining at least the probability of definable and characteristic types of events. These forces act inside of a man's body and psyche as well as in the whole universe, yet from the usual astrological point of view they have their source in outer space; their operations can be determined by a study of the periodical movements of the planets and possibly by the characteristics of certain sections of galactic space.

Thus meditation is supposed to draw the attention of the mind and the feelings towards the center of a person's bieng, while astrology provides knowlege through the rational and consistent study of man's "cosmic environment."

However, so to define both meditation and astrology makes it difficult to grasp the deeper or fuller significance of both these ap-proaches. The most perfect meditation is one which encompasses every moment of individual existence; it has become a never-relinquished *attitude* toward individual existence. Every act, every thought, every feeling can be experienced as successive phases in a lifelong process of self-knowledge and meaningful self-actuali-zation. And the knowledge of the state of the surrounding universe and the interplay of planetary and stellar cycles at every moment of an individual's life can be seen by the true astrologer to be but a decoding of a profound "Mystery language" whose every word is formed on the luminous screen of a consciousness, for which there can be no difference between Above and Below, the universe and the person. There can be no difference because, to the true astrologer's mind, what astrology studies is *not* the "influences" of celestial bodies upon earthly biophysical man but rather the ever-changing "form" which the immense and multifarious play of existence assumes in the consciousness of either collective mankind or the individual person.

When planets and stars are not only visualized but experienced, moving ceaselessly in a magnificent dance of existence, how could it be said that astrology deals with *external* forces or influences? And as any meditation in which consciousness does not move from the individual to the whole of which the individual is a functional part can only lead to a subtle glorification of the status of individuality, how could the true meditation fail to lead to a serene and harmonious ritual of self-universalization?

Meditation may rightfully begin with an inward movement of consciousness, and it is astrology's true nature to begin with a contemplative study of the sky and its hieroglyphs of light on the vast parchment of night. But in both instances this is only the beginning. Meditation and astrology can and should meet in their ultimate stance, at which point the individual becomes the whole (meditation) and the cosmic whole is sensed and perceived as a play performed within the illumined field of a freely focused individual consciousness.

Then there can no longer be any question as to whether the sky is the symbol and the individual person the real, or the person is the symbol and the universe reality. Because meditation had dissolved the ego, and astrology had focused planets and stars within the vibrant field of a personality that is both totally open and precisely focused, the symbolic and the real can be fused in a total experience of being.

88

The often so harshly disputed issue of whether or not astrology can present us with the certainty, the probability or only the possibility of future events is, as I see it, rather irrelevant. There are really no such things as future events; there are only as yet unactualized phases of our existence. What we call rather crudely "events" are opportunities to become step-by-step what we potentially are.

There are opportunities of various types, and astrology classifies these according to a twelvefold scheme. One may think of the twelve "houses" of an astrological chart as colors which, when experienced all at once in their dynamic interplay become the pure light of consciousness; but such analogies can be more confusing than helpful. What concerns us here is the possibility of focusing one's meditative approach upon a few essentials of living by following certain pathways which emerge from the very nature of astrological techniques when simplified to the extreme.

Simplification is here the keyword. There are a few great themes which appear in a multitude of variations in the lives of human beings wherever located. They should be taken into our consciousness and allowed to grow and mature. To each individual they appear under characteristic shapes and disguises. Each person's birth-chart can give significant clues to the reality underneath the disguise — and what we call events are indeed disguises. If we face them intently and without fear or prejudice, if we break through the obscuring veils of Isis, we find that they all are as yet unknown or long forgotten faces of our individual selfhood.

What our birth-chart should reveal to us are outlines of our usually unfamiliar self, our celestial Name. There is nothing to do with it save to use one feature of it after the other as paths that, if we follow them intently in our meditation, may lead us to the mystical Diamond Soul within which the pure light of consciousness is found, and from which this light radiates in many and wondrous colors.

In this small book some of these potential pathways to the light of an eventual fulfillment in consciousness and wisdom have been briefly outlined. In so doing, my purpose has not been to intellectualize about astrology concepts but rather to stimulate the intuition and challenge the capacity latent in every man to ask questions. And the first question is naturally: Who am I? — a question which can be asked in different ways and lead to varied answers according to the general frame of reference which any culture provides for the growing child.

The themes for meditation which are offered here follow in a general sense the sequence of the twelve astrological houses — which must not be confused or identified with the signs of the zodiac, and which indeed have nothing to do with the zodiac, whether of signs or constellations. The sequence is basic in terms of personal growth and self-fulfillment. Astrology, especially in its psychological and humanistic aspect identifies the houses with the twelve sections of the space surrounding any new emergence of organic life and consciousness; and by so doing it relates to the whole universe the development of a man's capacity to experience as "I" whatever the process of meeting the various aspects of his biopsychic environment brings to his central consciousness. This development of the capacity to experience as "I" operates through the lifelong ritual of self-actualization. It starts from the point of view of the narrowly conditioned ego — a social-cultural construct required for everyday living. At a higher turn of the spiral, marked by a 7-year and 28-year rhythm, it may proceed in terms of the self, the Power within, the Godseed in every human being. The end then is "self-universalization," the cosmification of individual existence.

Meditation has been defined in many ways. Essentially it always has to do with the use of the mind in the attempt to change the frame of reference within which this mind operates. this frame of reference is set in childhood by both the drives of the biopsychic nature of man, and the basic images, concepts, modes of expression and feeling-values which any child absorbs from his family, culture and society. Language, culture and tradition are needed at first to form the mind, just as the embryo needs a womb to mature into. But what was necessary at first becomes the most basic obstacle to overcome. The sequence of the twelve astrological houses symbolizes the archetypal process of both enjoying and overcoming.

The mind itself must be overcome and transcended; but what is to be overcome and transcended are its limitations and above all its polarization. The mind should be *repolarized*. Symbolically speaking it must no longer be the servant of the Sun, but instead the "agent" of the Galaxy. This is self-universalization. The consciousness reaches beyond the realm of dependence upon *specific forms* of cognition and experiencing. It reaches a condition in which practically any form of experience and communication is possible — a realm of pure potentiality.

One may say then that it is God now who acts *through* the person; but if one thinks of God as a "specific form" one misses the whole point. No "one" acts. There is action. There is existence — existence rhythmically flowing out of and into an infinite Ocean of potentiality.

Meditation, yes. But the word means everything and nothing. It can be a crutch. It can be release. It may be joy, peace, certainty, love, illumination. It may be silence that is frighteningly total, the voiding of all possibilities of frames of reference. It may last five minutes, a second, a lifetime. To meditate is to live at every instant at the threshold of one's greater being — one's galactic being.

"Who Am I?"

In recent years this most basic of all questions has been aksed again and again by young and no-so-young men and women distraught by the confusion, the conflicts, the pervasive insecurity of our present-day "human conditions." All over the world, sensitive individuals and traditional groups still hugging crumbling idols and institutions are experiencing what it is now fashionable to call an identity-crisis. They ask: Who am I? Yet what they actually mean in most cases is *what* am I?

Identity simply means being something that exists with a particular character different from all its environment — distinct, definable, nameable, standing in its own space with a rhythm of its own, "doing its own thing." The keynote here is the word, different. You realize that you feel differently from people around you, especially your family, your business associates and Mr. Average-citizen. You think differently, you wish to act differently — in your own way. But *what* is "your own way?" You try to define this "your own." And as you try to formulate to yourself this *what,* you may stop and wonder: "But *who* am I?" And there is no answer. Not for a long time. Until some experience, perhaps suddenly, opens a door hidden in some dark corner of your consciousness.

What is "seen" through the door may differ greatly with different persons. To some it is a blinding light; to others a deep darkness that draws. A few individuals may feel a beautiful, exalting Presence that speaks to them. Others may move boldly through the door and find themselves in a new environment — a new realm of consciousness and of relationship. A new sense of "belonging" comes upon them. *They have been accepted into the universe.*

What does it mean to have been accepted into the universe? They should come to realize that it means, first of all, that *they* have accepted their place and function in the universe. And this place and function may have very little to do with what their family, school, society not only expected of them but usually sought by all available means — some physical, other psychological — to impress indelibly upon their helpless organism during infancy and childhood.

Neither parents nor society constitute the whole universe. The womb that conditioned the growth of the embryo which became "you," the individual person, was not the whole universe. The society which seeks to train rigidly your mind so that you may fit into specific business or military patterns is not the whole universe. You were born out of your mother's womb. It is only as you experience "rebirth" out of that other matrix — your culture and your society — that you can know *who* you are.

You must be reborn into the sky, into the universe. Your reborn self is your true self; it is who you are in relation to the whole universe, the pattern of your true identity.

This pattern is your astrological birth-chart. It has been within you since your first breath; but you could not see it, because you were still held within the enfolding power — and the possessive love — of your close environment. Now it can speak to you. It delivers to you the message of the sky — your celestial Name.

Your Celestial Identity

One of the most basic steps in the process of self-actualization through meditation is to distinguish as clearly as you can between *what* you are and *who* you are. The "what" defines the complex set of activities, functions, instincts, drives and desires which in their interrelations constitute your own nature. They refer to what is called by people around you your temperament, your character. However, these biopsychic urges and activities are in a constant state of flux. They wax and wane in intensity. They interact at times in a harmonious manner, at other times in ways which lead to frictions and perhaps conflict, because your total energy is limited and all these basic organic activities try to draw to themselves a greater part of this energy. They also compete for the attention of your ego. Very often indeed your ego-consciousness which should reflect the state of the whole organism identifies itself instead with only one or the other of these drives — the most active, the most dominant or insecure. It fears; it is angry or depressed; it loves; it experiences anxiety and a sense of isolation or frustration.

Neither one of these biopsychic urges, nor the ego which somehow tries or appears to control the "field" in which they operate — i.e., your total personality — is "who" you are. "You" are not even the whole field. You are this field *in relation to the universe.*

The names which you have been given by your parents in terms of some cultural tradition or personal bias refer to what you appear to be to others, and most of the time to yourself. They represent what you are as a *social* being. On the other hand, your birth-chart symbolizes what you are as a *celestial* being, a citizen of the universe. To which will you choose to respond?

In your birth-chart the ten planets (including Sun and Moon) refer to the "what you are." They are the letters of your Name. however, as you grow up, everyday their positions in the sky change, their interrelationship is also altered. The solar system is their field of activity; it represents your personality as a whole and its basic functions, psychic as well as physical.

But there are many people born on the same day. "Who am I, then?" you will ask. The particular way you and the universe face each other; that is to say, your precise orientation to this universe. As the Earth rotates around its axis, at every point of the globe and at every moment of the day this orientation takes on a particular character. This character is defined in astrology by the zodiacal positions of the horizon and the meridian at the exact moment of your first breath. These crossing horizontal and vertical lines in your birth-chart form a framework, not only within which, but in reference to which planets, stars, and all other factors operate. They define the fourfold structure of your individual existence, the foundations of your being — *who* you are.

The Interplay of Consciousness and Power

In the early days of ancient agricultural socieities, in China, Egypt, India, Mesopotamia, astrology was concerned with the rhythm of regularly repeating natural phenomena — with seasonal activity, with the start of the rise of great rivers which watered desertic lands, with the mating of animals, etc. Soon it began to deal with matters affecting the tribe or the kingdom at a social and military level. Astrologers erected charts for the beginning of a king's reign; only later did they study the birth-moment of the king, and still later of prominent personages.

In the big cities of the pre-Christian era birth-charts were cast for many individuals of the wealthy class, and the practice flourished during the European Renaissance and thereafer. Every court had its astrologer. To predict events and select the best time to start some enterprise was the main business of the astrologer. It still is so today for the majority of them. This is the popular aspect of astrology.

Only very recently has astrology been used deliberately as a technique for furthering the psychological development of individual persons, that is, the process of "individuation" or "self-actualization." This is the "person-centered" type of astrology — what might be called *cosmopsychology*. Such an astrology can be used as a basis for the type of meditation that seeks to establish an individual's status in the universal whole, thus the foundation of his original and true being at the present moment of time and human evolution.

In order to make this use constructive, we have first of all to have a clear grasp of what a birth-chart is essentially a circle divided into four basic sections by the cross of horizon and meridian. The circle represents a two-dimensional projection of the celestial sphere, i.e., of *our* universe. We are born at the center of it. We live in it part of the time in a horizontal position, part of the time standing up.

In astrological symbolism the horizontal line refers to the factor of *consciousness:* consciousness of self at the eastern or dawn point, called the Ascendant — consciousness of our relationship to other selves (and to the outer world in general) at the western or sunset point, the Descendant. The vertical line of the chart (the meridian) symbolizes *power;* and power is always the result of a process of integration and concentration of energies. At the bottom of the chart, the process of integration deals with the growth of psychic roots, the home, the building of personality. The upper end of the vertical axis of the birth-chart refers to the public or social life and profession, i.e., to the manner in which we integrate ourselves in our community.

Consciousness and power are the two poles of human existence. Consciousness tranforms potentiality into power; but through the use of power — in Sanskrit *shakti* — new forms of consciousness arise which in turn actualize a new quantum of energy from the vast ocean of potentiality out of which universes periodically emerge. This is the great Play of existence — the cyclic interaction of *Yin* and *Yang,* in Chinese philosophy. You are an individualized aspect of this eternal "dialogue" of consciousness and power.

Can you learn to feel and see yourself in such a manner? It will be difficult at first; but you should keep such a realization in the background of your mind — yes, underneath the ever-changing patterns and problems of your everyday life.

As you see yourself as symbolized primarily by the constant interaction of horizon and meridian, you may gain a new sense of individuality. Wherever you go you always are the interaction of horizontal consciousness and vertical power. You are the center of their cross of individual existence, the Rose that blooms where the two lines meet. This Rose is the true "Heart center" of man.

The Individual's Word of Power

Astrology is a language. If you understand this language, the sky speaks to you. It tells you what you were born for and how you can best actualize the potentialities of your own nature. This is the most important thing you can ever know, i.e., how to become fully what is possible for you to be, how to fulfill your place in the universe. You should do this consciously and through the intelligent use of power.

As you look at your birth-chart, calculated for the exact moment and place of your breath, your attention should be drawn first to the ends of the horizontal and vertical lines. These are the four Angles of the chart.

The Ascendant (to the left of the chart) tells you what sign and degree of the zodiac were rising at the eastern horizon when you began to breathe. This is a very sacred point, for it represents the dawn of your consciousness, the signature of what you are as a self, the keynote of your individuality. More than any single factor in a birth-chart, it tells you *who* you are as a person with a relatively unique function in the universe (destiny). Unfortunately it is not easy in most cases to be certain of the exact moment of one's first breath. But if one knows at least the approximate time one can often "rectify" the chart and discover what the exact moment was, and thus the exact zodiacal degree of the Ascendant.

The Ascendant is just as important as the Sun in your birth-chart. The popular idea that one "is" Aries, Taurus, Leo, etc., is fallacious. The Sun in a chart refers to the basic quality of the life-energy within a human organism; it indicates, one might say, the type of fuel on which the engine of personality runs. This evidently is a basic factor; but it deals only with the foundations of the temple of your individual being. The zodiacal sign and degree of the Ascendant tells you the basic character and purpose of the temple — what it is built for — your most intimate relationship with the universe.

As you meditate upon your Ascendant you should not do it as if it were an isolated factor. It must never be separated from the Descendant — its opposite point in the zodiac — nor from the two ends of the vertical axis of the chart, which (at least symbolically) refer to the nadir and zenth — the roots and the flowering of your individual existence. Selfhood (Ascendant) cannot be separated from the capacity for relationship (Descendant); and consciousness (horizon) remains ineffectual without the power to express it through an integrated personality (nadir) and through some form of participation in a community, small or large (zenith).

Your birth-chart is a "word of power." Like the Hebrew sacred Word, the Tetragrammation, it has four basic letters, its four Angles. They are the basic consonants. The ten "planets" in your chart are the vowels, symbolizing the vibratory energies of *your* universe. Indeed, astrology is a sacred language. It establishes a basic form of communication between the universe and your own consciousness. But you have to learn the secret of silent listening which as well means seeing with truly open eyes. Quiet down your ego-mind and the voices of senses and emotions. Listen to the utterance of the Sky. It speaks in patterns of light projected upon the dark screen of the cosmos.

Selfhood is Destiny

Self is what is at the source of all individualized existence. It is inherent in the original Tone of being, the AUM. It is "rhythm," and it is also in latency "form." It is the Word that was in the beginning, and, in this Word, there is power as well as meaning. But the meaning at first is only latent; it has to become actualized through a long series of developments of vital energy and multitudes of experiences which gradually are seen by the mind to have a basic consistency; that is, they are felt to refer to a center of consciousness, to an "I."

Destiny is simply the structure of the process of existence which enables the newborn organism to develop in due time and after many steps and crises a consciousness of the vast set of potentialities inherent in its selfhood. Destiny is the way in which what was latent at birth can *best* become actualized in a mature individual person. An individual human being is always in the making — or perhaps in the last stages of his life in the unmaking, if he has accepted a crucial failure of consciousness and succumbed to the aging process of the body — a usual occurrence, alas, because man tends to identify consciousness with power, and when physical power wanes the person lets go of consciousness as well.

There is nothing "fateful" in destiny, unless we fail to understand that the sequence of life-events is structured by the very power that makes us what we are as an individual. Destiny is individuality. Self as a unique form of human existence exists in space; destiny in time. Self-hood is being; destiny is becoming.

What we call individuality is the seed-pattern of our being, from the first moment of individual existence — the first breath, the AUM tone of our existence as a person operating within an open environment — to the moment of death. Destiny refers to the process of actualization of what was released at birth as potentiality — a potentialy limited and defined by the genetic code at the core of every one of our billions of cells, and as well by the pressures of our social, cultural, planetary and cosmic environment.

This process of destiny operates indeed under great pressures. A human being becomes an "individual person" under pressure and through the heat of many an encounter, in the same way in which coal can be transmuted into diamond. The fundamental question any human being has to answer, by his actions, his feelings and his thoughts, much more than by mere words of assent or despair, is: Do you accept to become diamond? Do you accept to be what you potentially were at birth, regardless of hardships, of apparent failures, of disintegrated ideals — which perhaps were only the reflections of someone else's ideals for you?

The pattern of destiny is *implied* in your birth-chart; but what is implicit has to be made explicit. Most human beings tire very early of the efforts to become what is implied in their *logos,* the Word that was in the beginning of their individual existence. They would rather follow the highway of conformity to family, social, cultural and always local ideas. Astrologically speaking, they are affected by "transits," i.e., by the pressures of what happens outside of them, in their society, in the universe.

What matters essentially, however, is for a man to allow the seed-pattern represented by his birth-chart to unfold its powers and develop its faculties according to the internal rhythms of his individual nature. This refers, at least partially, to what is called "progressions."

But progressions are not to be thought of as isolated incidents. They can only be understood, and should always be considered — if one meditates upon them — as an organic sequence of developments, as destiny revealing itself to the mind so that the consciousness may more fully understand their implications and cooperate with the external opportunities for personal transformation.

At this stage in the meditative process what is important is simply to try to feel the interplay of individuality and destiny, of permanent form and evolving form, of being and becoming. in order to pass victoriously through the twelve great tests of individual experience it is necessary to remain deeply aware of, and to have faith in what in us is permanent, that is, the unchanging tone of self and the fundamental structure of our individuality; but it is just as essential to meet change and personal transformations in a quiet and welcoming attitude of acceptance. This does not mean "resignation" in the old Christian sense. It does not mean either exuberance and over-optimism. Perhaps it can mean "love" — the love of the yet-unknown, just because it is unknown and knowable, because it essentially belongs to us, and we to it, as we belong to the universe which nevertheless is "our" universe.

And so, one moves on, open like a clear sky — watching the great dance of stars and planets, all within ourselves. Watching without fear, without expectation. *Letting* it all happen, yet being intensely aware, free to move in the direction of the wind of destiny, always different yet ever the same — as is the universe.

You Are Never Alone

Many individuals today experience, and complain of a poignant feeling of loneliness or alienation. Very few perhaps relate the word, solitude, to *sol,* meaning the sun. Again etymologically, "alone" means *all-one*. When men began to break away from the compulsive, because instinctual and biopsychic, matrix of their archaic type of tribal society; when they gathered into cities amid people to whom they were not related by blood, land or culture, they felt uprooted, exiled — "individuals" perhaps, but alone. Solitude was heavy to bear. Is that the price one must pay for being an in-dividual (i.e., indivisible) and "all-one"?

During the day the sun shines gloriously, but alone. As a sun he is *solus,* solitary, single, a glorious Individual. Yet every sun is also a star, one among many companion-stars within the vast expanse of the galaxy. The spiritually awake individual person may accept outwardly the role of being a sun to many planets circling around him; yet *in his heart* he knows himself to be a star, a small unit within a cosmic "commune." The sun must not feel alone, if "all-one" and indivisible; he has his individual work to perform in the galactic commune. A human being may have been uprooted from the dark soil which fed him, but if he has discovered his place in the celestial whole, if he knows his celestial Name, how could he be "alienated"? He knows where he belongs in the universe.

The first House of your birth-chart symbolizes the basic test of isolation and solitude which every true individual has had to meet. Will you experience your self "all one," or suffer and wilt in aloneness, with a gnawing sense of not-belonging, or alienation.

When the astrologer speaks of a house, he refers first of all to the zodiacal sign on its "cusp" — the cusp being the beginning of the house. This zodiacal sign determines the basic *quality* of the type of experience signified by that house. The Ascendant is the cusp of the first house, which is the 30-degree wide section of space just below the Eastern horizon at the time and place of the first breath. This first house as a whole deals with those experiences though which normally and in the most appropriate manner, the character of your individuality and your uniqueness of destiny will be revealed to you

One or more planets may have been located in this first house when you were born. Their nature will affect powerfully your *sense of self* and the way in which you will have to meet — or should meet, *for best results* — your emergence as an individual from maternal, social, religious and scholastic "wombs." If Mars is "rising" (i.e., just below the Eastern horizon) at your birth, you may have to struggle rather aggressively for self-identification, and the result may be, by reaction, a subsequent feeling of isolation. On the other hand, Venus in the first house of your birth-chart suggests a more harmonious, loving type of emergence — unless this Venus is affected by strongly discordant relationships with other planets. Sometimes it could be almost *too* harmonious. One can become bound by love to this or that matrix. Several planets in the first house mean a complex process of self-discovery influenced by perhaps contradictory factors or indicating a series of crises of emergence.

As you meditate on the contents of your first house do not become identified with these contents, whatever they are. They simply show you how to recognize more clearly opportunities for self-discovery when you meet them. A "rising planet" does not "do" anything to "you," the self. It is there to tell you how best to actualize your birth-potential. This actualization can take place at several levels — biological, psychological, mental. Just let it happen; but try to do so consciously and with a serene feeling of acceptance.

Carl Jung defined Tao as "the conscious way." This is indeed what astrology can and should be: a conscious way of growth, without fear or anticipation. Not looking forward nervously and anxiously to a projection into the future of our expectation, but recognizing and identifying experiences *as they come;* seeing them in their full meaning within our total destiny.

What Are Possessions For?

It is often said that "to be" is far more important than "to have"; and in terms of our usual idea of what "having" means this is indeed true. This truth is now being recognized by many young people in our posssessions-haunted America, and such a realization could transform our sacrosanct way of life. But, in a more fundamental sense, being implies having. If I assert that *I am*, it seems that "I" possess a body, a mind, a voice. "I" is only an abstraction if separated from "am."

In your astrological birth-chart, the second house, below the eastern horizon, refers to possessions; but this word, possessions, is usually thought of in a much too narrow sense; i.e., merely as money or goods. It should mean *anything* necessary to manifest in concreteness of existence what you are as an individual center of existence and consciousness; thus anything *through the use of which* you can "be" as a person. As you utter your first cry, various material substances and as well inherited faculties are there for you to use. Some men are born "poor," others "rich," in psychological and biological as well as social and financial ways. The most important spiritual fact of human existence, however, is not the amount or even the character of what you own, but the use you make of it. It is to this use of what is "yours" *by birth-right* that the astrological indications provided by the second house of your birth-chart (calculated for the precise moment and place of your first breath) refer.

You may use constructively, one pointedly and purposefully, as efficient managers, all that is yours by right of birth in a particular family, class, society; or you may squander your resources. What is more, you may use them, or they may use you! The lives of many people are controlled by what they own — or by the lack of possessions. They are controlled by social status, by what society expects a man or woman should do with these possessions; and this includes the person's body, sexual attractiveness, male strength —and even the intellectual capacities inherited from well-educated parents. You can be a slave to traditions and family patterns of behavior.

Astrology does *not* deal with quantity, only with qualitative values and efforts, Jupiter in your natal second house need not mean that you were born rich, or if Saturn is there, poor. The planets in that house refer to the kind of use you make of whatever you own, be it much or little; and, even more basically, to your *attitude* toward any form of ownership. Saturn may make you fearful of loss or clinging jealously to your possessions. Jupiter can show generosity and an at least relative feeling of abundance. It tends to reveal good managerial abilities. But the spiritual issue in this case is whether the person manages his inner or outer wealth as a trustee for mankind, or for his own self-aggrandizement. Mars in this second house tends to show a relatively constant outflow of financial resources or inherited abilities. What is owned is readily mobilized for use, but perhaps also impulsively squandered. Venus in that House suggests the ability to profit from cultural or group values, to make everything you own fructify.

Seek always to assess truthfully, unemotionally and without glamor or false modesty the values of what you have. Try to exteriorize this value, yet without show or pride. Sloppiness can be physical or psychological and intellectual. Every individual has the responsibility to exemplify an ideal of value. There is always someone who, witnessing this example, will find in himself an as yet unrealized source of inner or outer wealth. The keynote here is simplicity; the shadow, ostentatiousness.

Your Environment and You

A man may be thought of as an individual soul manifesting in and through a body, but even the religious persons are coming to realize that you cannot in fact separate the individual from his natal environment. This is not to say that a man is "the creature of his environment." It only means that individual and environment are two constantly interacting factors.

The individual person is born in a social as well as biological and planetary environment. If we believe in some form of reincarnation — whether of a transcendent Soul or a bundle of "karmic tendencies" — whatever is born needed the exact kind of environment in which it is born, and the environment needed as well this new being. Every newborn has a potential function to perform in the total evolution of mankind and of the Earth; and he is born at that time and place because he needs the life-conditions they provide to the fulfillment of his Karma or Soul-purpose.

The third house and its contents refer traditionally to whatever a newborn finds around him. It was particularly connected with "brothers and sisters" and all near-relatives, but this is obviously a simplification. What is meant is essentially the type of experience which arises daily from contacts with other human beings with whom one is related by blood, culture and social tradition. In polar opposition to this type of experience, the ninth house refers to experiences involving long journeys, contacts with foreigners and all relationships the character of which implies a remote, generalized or transcendent ideal of association.

Here again what the psychologically oriented type of astrologer has in mind is not so much a description of what the child meets around his earliest steps, but his attitude toward these meetings and their results upon the development of his thinking and feelings. The young child receives an immense variety of impressions to which he reacts; and his reactions are at first in terms of self-preservation and adjustments. The latter involves cunning, the most primitive form of intelligence; that is, the ability to use other people to bring pleasure and avoid discomfort or pain.

Intelligence at this stage is purely self-centered. It seeks to make of all environmental factors — people, animals, nature in general — a secure, thus integrated, whole of which the child is the center, at least in his own consciousness. If he cannot succeed in this instinctive purpose, he often withdraws into an imaginary world, plays with unseen playmates, etc.

Today many people's thoughts are drawn to ecological prolems. Our society has insidiously poisoned our natural enviroment. What can we do to survive successfully in it? Shall we react by moving to as yet unspoiled places, living on the fringe of our relentless society and building our own ideal world as small groups of imaginative individuals — or should we try to change this deleterious greed-infested Western civilization by all possible means? But what kind of means; organized sociopolitical action or sporadic explosive violence? Some children are extraordinarily clever at playing father against mother, sister against brother, becoming the center of attraction and decision; others go into tantrums and become neurotic — another way of getting attention, and also of exerting revenge.

As always the question to meditate upon is what your attitude should be when meeting problems caused by your environment. Some problems seem strictly personal; yet we are all involved in collective or group patterns of existence. We are caught in the karmic wheels of history. Our birth-chart may suggest not so much a way *out* as a way *through*. Intelligence is the way.

The Ecological Approach To Knowledge

Intelligence is the ability to adjust to one's environment so that one may extract from it *optimal* conditions for personal growth and creative self-fulfillment. But there are various ways of "adjusting." What is to be adjusted actually is the *relationship* between the individual person and the social and natural environment. This relationship should be "just" or "right" — thus fulfilling and not impairing the essential nature of either the individual or the environment.

Unfortunately our Biblical tradition has promoted a basically unsound attitude toward the environment: man alone is worthwhile, and all that surrounds him is there for him to master as he pleases. When this drive to mastery pervades intelligence and dominates the mechanisms of the mind, tragedy is the end-result. We have reached that stage.

This puts in question the whole concept of knowledge. It forces us to distinguish between "optimum" and "maximum" in terms of knowledge — between the best and the most. Making such a distinction is certainly dangerous; but not making it may be even more dangerous. It should be made in terms of intelligence and not of the proud urge for mastery which Western civilization still officially glorifies as the one means for achievement and success. But what is "success"?

Lincoln said that insofar as he refused to be the slave of any master, he likewise refused to be a master of slaves. Mastery is based on the use of power; and we say that "knowledge is power." But is there not an optimum value to power, beyond which its use will be destructive to all concerned, including the user? Only "intelligence" can determine this optimum value; and this means

110

that what is to be considered is *the relationship* between the individual and nature (or society), and NOT the craving of the individual for power and mastery over his natural and social environment.

Intelligence leads to wisdom; intellect to knowledge. Wisdom implies the ability to understand when to stop in an action which endangers *the relationship* between the self and the not-self, between man and nature. Man should transform nature by cultivation and domestication, but only as far as the transformation does not endanger the ecological harmony of the whole biosphere. How to learn "how far" one can go?

As the young child comes in contact with brothers, sisters, friends, animals and the to him confusing world of adults, he learns *how far* he can go without incurring punishment or pain. Will our society, acting as an ill-tempered child seeking to dominate his family circle, learn to be intelligent in dealing with his planetary environment? Will it cease racing after an intellectual and analytical knowledge geared to the drive for a kind of power which it has been unable to use without destroying itself and nature?

An individual may often learn from his birth-chart what is his best approach to the development of intelligence — that is, the attitude and the type of situations which lead to a most wholesome adjustment to his environment. When his natal third house contains planets, these usually indicate the best line to pursue in the attainment of the most primary type of knowledge.

What Is Education For?

The validity of our traditional European type of education is being challenged rather brutally. Why? Because it is geared to the perpetuation of a past which has led to a ghastly situation in spite of all the material abundance and comfort lavished upon the majority of Americans. What we still call "education" is in fact mainly "instruction." The teacher seeks to impress a mass of data and formulas upon young minds and to instill into them certain traditional methods of evaluating and relating these data — i.e., a particular approach to the acquisition of knowledge.

There is nothing "wrong" about this, provided one believes that this particular approach and the use we generally make of the knowledge gained in schools and universities are truly constructive in a deeply *human* sense. The trouble is, however, that this belief may not be justified. Many people today earnestly feel and indeed logically think that our traditional Western mentality and many typically American attitudes to life, knowledge and spiritual unfoldment are based on assumptions which should be radically transformed. As a result we are truly witnessing what is now widely called a "revolution in consciousness."

Consciousness develops in the infant by virtue of his contacts with his psychic as well as physical environment. It is affected not only by what the people around him do and the feelings they express, but by the collective mentality of the society and the special class in which he is born. This collective mentality is the insistent background on which the child's intelligence develops. In an astrological birth-chart the third house refers to *the relationship* between the child's inherent, but at first only potential, individuality and this collective mentality. The planets in this natal third house — and the zodiacal sign on its cusp — should give valuable indications concerning the character of this relationship.

A planet in a house reveals the problems as well as the opportunities which the individual person has to grow through the type of experiences which this house symbolizes. A characteristic case was that of the famous biologist Pasteur in whose chart we find seven planets in the natal third house. His attention was focused upon his relationship with the collective mentality of his time. He reacted in many and forceful ways to what was then traditional scientific knowledge; and his work and his name are immortalized by every bottle of pasteurized milk sold today and by the asepticism of modern surgical procedures.

A truly "human," rather than culture bound, education would give the child constant opportunities to challenge his tradition and the validity of the data and the methods he is taught. Surely, he should know the essential features of what mankind *as a whole* — and not only our Western civilization — has believed, thought, felt and practiced. He should know them because he is the end-result of this millennial human past. But he should never be made to take for granted that the solution to the many problems of existence which have been proposed were necessarily correct. He should be urged not only to question the implied postulates of Western science, morality and religiosity, but to seek creative ways toward a new life and a society encompassing all men everywhere.

Today we see being stressed over and over the fact that education should be an unending process in a period of intense and swift social, economic and intellectual changes. But this is primarily a quantitative way of looking at the situation. It is the *quality* of the education process which is important. What you want to gain is knowledge the quality of which enables you to fulfill more consciously and productively your individual destiny. Try to feel deeply and without emotional prejudices what is the quality of knowledge that you need most to play your part in this revolutionary age.

The Foundations of Personality

In the first house of a birth-chart we see what constitutes the uniqueness of the individual, and more precisely *the best way* in which the newborn will discover who he is as an individual — the exact zodiacal degree of the Ascendant suggesting even more specifically, though of course symbolically, *who* he is. But this "who," at the level of the Ascendant, is only a potentiality. The potential has to become concrete and actualized in a living, operating, feeling organism, the individual "person." This process of concretization works out through experiences related to the second and third houses of the natal chart, i.e., through the experience of owning a body and things, and through the need to adjust to the environment. It is particularly defined and stabilized by the experiences which relate to the fourth house.

The main characteristic of the intellect is to seek to contact and analyze everything. Modern man suffers from an exaggerated avidity for intellectualized knowlege. "More, more!" seems to be the battle cry of the Western mind craving to touch, violate, and reduce to analytical and statistically based concepts all that his senses and his machines may reach. A time must come when the confusion of knowledge becomes such that it is imperative to stop to go inward and downward — to experience restraint, self-containment, stability. Then man is tested by life. Everything in the future will depend on when, where and how he is impelled to stop. Where he stops, there he realizes the essential *foundations of his personality*. From these foundations he will go forth, expressing himself, meeting others and facing the world at large. To advance in height requires a foundation in depth.

However there are superficial and deep foundations. There are trees whose roots spread widely below the surface of the soil;

others have very deep taproots. There are houses which are solid by being strongly structured, yet almost floating over the earth-surface, like ships. Is your mind stable, your emotions well-balanced? Most people find stability — which means as well inner security — by being deeply rooted in a social and religious tradition. Their ancestry is a strong tree of which they are a branch, small or large. But what happens if the earth itself shakes and the roots are loosened, or the trunk snaps under the violence of a hurricane?

At such times a person experiences a real identity-crisis. The crisis is inevitably based on a more or less crucial change in the individual's relationship to that which has molded, or at least defined, his growth and brought him a sense of security. Any life-foundation which is the product of a static form of stability and security may either become irrelevant and unacceptable to the growing person, or be radically shaken by historical-social or telluric cataclysms. Even the house built on a rock can be shattered by an earthquake or a tornado.

A truly reliable and quake-proof stability comes only to him who has reached center; who has become a global being, who has attained planetary consciousness. At the center of the globe there is peace; gravitation is negated. The centers of all spheres through the whole universe are mysteriously linked in a cosmic Brotherhood.

The fourth house, and the nadir point of the chart symbolize the basic stability of individual existence. This house has been traditionallly associated with the home and in most cases the mother, for the mother symbolizes the ancestral continuum of life, pure conservatism, the "inertia" of the being seeking to remain what it has been since its very beginning. But the fourth house has a broader meaning. It refers to whatever represents for an individual the roots, or the center, of his actual being as a person. Try to experience in your meditation what you are ready to accept — to accept unquestionably — as the foundations of your individual person. The fourth house of your chart and what it may contain should give you clues to the best manner in which you can reach center — and thus become truly a citizen of the universe.

"Express Yourself": What Self?

In our society which brandishes the words self-expression, freedom, creativity as if they were flags to be raised on the ruins of old edifices on conformity, the main issues are easily forgotten. One should try to let these strident voices die out. In the silence of meditation one should seek to pierce through the glamour of battle-cries of vehement desires and to uncover the hidden question marks which words and slogans so easily hide.

Ex-pression means "pressing outward," just as emotion implies a motion aiming at reaching some outside object or goal. When we speak of creativity we have in mind the exteriorization or projection of an internal state of feeling or mental awareness. And the drive toward freedom never occurs unless we feel in some manner bound, even if it is only by traditional attitudes and beliefs which have ceased to be relevant, just, and guarantees of security and peace. Rarely is any mention made of *what* or *who* is eager to press outward, to move toward some intensely desired object or ideal, to project itself or himself into a work of art, a new song, an invention, a deed. What is it that feels bound and yearns not to feel bound, perhaps regardless of what this "liberated" status will mean and lead to?

In the immense majority of cases it is not the self. It is the ego or, as often, some particular biopsychic drive inherent in human nature which for a moment has gained control of the ruling seat of consciousness and proclaimed itself "I" — I want; I must have; I must be satisfied. And in this lies the illusive, if not fallacious or even tragic character of so much that goes under the banner of self-expression and liberation — even of creativity.

116

Through experiences which fall into the fifth house category, a person releases energy, theoretically in order to satisfy a desire, but actually in most cases simply because energy has built up within the force field of his personality and it must find an outlet for release. If it does not find it, there may be an explosion, or some sort of organic or psychic deterioration may set in. But what does one mean by "outlet"? Must it be an *outlet,* or could it be an *inlet*?

The essential issue here is what we mean by self. In current psychological practice the word, self, is used as if it meant the person; and there is no clear distinction between self and ego. The result is a confusion of values. When self-expression actually means a release of emotional energy just for the sake of release, with little or no concern for how the energy let out will affect the objects or the persons receiving its impact, it should be called ego-expression.

The results of the release may be beautiful, inspiring. Yet in a universe in which everything is related to everything else, and where any action inevitably produces a reaction which sooner or later will rebound upon the actor, this ego-expression is likely to backfire. It can be considered truly valuable only when its effects upon other human beings and the environment as a whole can also be shown to be valuable.

In childhood and youth the results of one's actions upon other people are rarely taken in consideration. The biological instinct for acting out one's moods, desires or whims is usually overpowering. The purpose of education along the lines of a particular way of life and culture is to introduce in the consciousness a concern with the character and the end-results of one's actions. Yet the socialization of the ego merely tends to substitute devious procedures for the spontaneous outflow of the youth's emotional desires. Hypocrisy replaces the youth's ebullience.

As we seek to use in our meditation factors involved in fifth house types of activity we should ask ourselves these questions:

Where do I stand as a source of energy-release? Is it right for me, consciously or unconsciously, to impress forcibly upon the world the biopsychic energies which, having become stabilized within the "engine" of my personality, have become productive of excess power? Do I "express myself" without regard to other people's needs and reactions, really not caring what happens as long as I can be delivered from what the Romantic philosopher, Nietzsche, called "the unbearable torment of my plenitude?" Is it even *really* excess energy; and might it not be only the result of having been conditioned by my environment, by social fashion or the special mores of my class or group? Am I sure that what my society and culture made me, or what I made myself, perhaps in protest, is a valuable example I should want to impress upon my children, friends or associates?

What the cusp of your fifth house proves to be, and whether or not the house contains planets, will not answer these questions. But it should give you a clue as to *where and how to find the answers.* If, for instance, you have Mars in your fifth house, this does not mean that it is natural and wonderful for you to rush out toward all you desire externally. Neither does it make you a gambler or a Don Juan. It points out to you that in your natural eagerness to act out what you inwardly are as an individual person, you should pay special attention to the *quality of the energy* you will be releasing when you express yourself — thus to the intrinsic character, rhythm and purity of this energy. If on the other hand, you have Venus in the fifth house, consider closely the value of your *motives* in wanting to create, to have children, to fulfill your emotional yearnings. Do not take the commonplace or traditional type of motivation as "good enough" for you. You should be willing to stand up consciously, personally for your values, as you try to externalize and objectify them through your actions.

With Jupiter and Saturn in your fifth house, you are warned to pay special attention to the social, religious, perhaps financial conditions in your environment which may stimulate or restrict your eagerness to give a special social background to your individual status when you take the initiative to show the world who you are. There is nothing wrong in wanting to express the type of self which finds its fulfillment in terms of normal social relationships and great collective ideals or forms of discipline, as long as you have consciously made them *your own.* Especially in the meditative approach to astrology a planet in a house does not tell you what to do, as much as how to go about doing it.

A truly "cosmopsychological" astrology seeks to make of the individual psyche a cosmos, that is a significant form of order. The emphasis is on *meaning.* Thus in the fifth house the individual should try to pay great attention to the motives, the right order, the value, the capacity for transformation (Uranus especially) and the fundamental significance (Pluto) of his attempts at self-expression.

"My Children": Really?

In our present-day society in which the generation gap has become such a poignant and at times tragic feature it is more important indeed that parents and parents-to-be should consider with utmost seriousness their motive for having children, and particularly their basic relationship to their children. Are the children "theirs"? Will the mother, subtly or crudely, feel still that her child is "the flesh of my flesh," and the father take for granted that his boy is meant to prolong his at least social pattern of life, insuring a kind of genetic immortality?

Children, except for very rare cases, are conceived under circumstances showing little or no conscious intent. Sperm and ovum blend in a process upon which the man and woman have no control. The most they can do is to stop using contraceptives when they decide that it would be nice to have a child. Evidently, the woman may experience a deep biological yearning for a child; the father may want to be the proud father of a son. This is the glamour with which the life of the species surrounds its basic drive for self-perpetuation.

A specific society, with its particular culture, religion and way of life, also seeks to perpetuate itself. It generates a collective urge for procreation among its members, an urge that in the past has been intensified by moral or financial rewards for a large family.

Thus the motivation for having a progeny has biological and cultural foundations, at least until the present time obsessed with the vision of a suicidal population explosion. Above these foundations, in our age of emotional problems and social chaos, the desires of individual men and especially women for having "their" children has become an essential part of the procreative motive.

Young people want children for psychological reasons. Producing a child becomes either a form of self-expression, or serves the purpose of making more concrete the man-woman union — a union which has lost its intrinsic sense of social permanence and therefore may need to be shored up and outwardly demonstrated to prove its solidity and worth.

As this occurs the relationship between the parents and the children takes on a "personalized" character which is bound to cause tensions in proportion as the old traditional relationship — based on the archetypes of Father, Mother, Child — loses its binding significance at the social and religious level. In olden days children belonged to the community, a community which represented a specific aspect of the human race. The parents were merely the unconscious carriers of ovum and sperm. The children were molded by the way of life of the community and the cultural patterns of self-perpetuating groups, clans or classes. The personal attachment of the parents to their children constituted only an overtone which, just in special cases and under psychological stresses, took on a dominant feature.

The situation today is almost completely changed. The relationship parents-children is almost totally "psychologized," creating therefore incessant problems. Parents living in a state of overt or barely controlled tension *use* the child in their game of one-up-manship. Emotional conflicts between the parents are thrown upon the children. The father and mother do not wish to act any longer as archetypes. They are eager to act as "persons" in relation to their children; they want to be chums, confidents, equals — or else they are too busy or too upset to care; which creates a psychological void in the child, a negative relationship.

As a result children are drawn together in surburban or school "peer groups." In our age of abundance they are given not only permissive independence, but money. They become potential customers for specialized products. An amoral business world sees to it that teen-agers or even smaller children are made into special groups with special interests. This isolates them from the "adult" generation. As several age-strata are publicized, related to characteristic interests and desire for sellable products, stereotyped patterns of collective response are deliberately produced and encouraged for business purposes.

Where do you stand in such a stratified, disorganic, conflict-ridden society? Your relationship to your children, your emotional possessiveness, your on-and-off concern for their welfare, your pride in them often gives a basic and more generalized clue. The quality of your desire for a child — the first one, or another to keep company to the first so that he or she is less bothersome — often indeed tells a great deal about the quality of your desire for self-expression. We live in a society of egos, by egos and for the greater glory of egos. Your children know it and see through your glamour-coated statements and ambiguous gestures, cocktails of love and annoyance. Can you be honest with them, and with your desires?

You may be the exception; but exceptions are not born, they are made — which means the exercise of "will." The fifth house has much to do with the quality of the will. Will is mobilization of energy; and emotion is likewise the mobilization of a feeling. "Behind will stands desire"; this is an old occult axiom. Everything therefore depends upon the quality of our desires; but this quality in turn depends upon the person's capacity to *image forth* the deeper longing of his or her true selfhood.

What is at stake is therefore in most cases the development of the imagination along lines which transcend the possessiveness inherent in *all* biological and egocentric drives. The function of great spiritual Teachers and Avatars, and even of geniuses who are deeply responsive to the advancing tide of human evolution, is therefore to stimulate the imagination of people around them, so that the quality of their desires may be raised to a state of incandescence, generating a powerful will for self-rebirth.

Learning Through Crises

A crisis is the opportunity to make a decision. A decision about what? About the quality of our desires and our actions. About the level from which your consciousness operates as it seeks to realize the significance of what has occurred or is happening to us.

The tragic thing in human life is that most people, when faced with a crisis — or what they call a crisis — do not take the opportunity of deciding to meet life, events and people from a different level of consciousness. They suffer through the crisis, but the suffering comes to nothing; it is all in vain. Men go to war, are tortured, experience severe illness, personal humiliation, loss of love or fortune; yet they do not fundamentally change. Life afterward goes on "as usual." There are scars, scars of so often useless victories or meaningless defeats, but no radical transformation. What is experienced is confusion, rather than a new level of communication, a new feeling toward work, a more inspired sense of service to mankind.

It has been said that the only illness is to be ill for no purpose. The only tragedy is to pass through a crucial crisis in vain, for futile reasons and with meaningless results. Science fiction writers tell tales of adventures to galactic realms, of world catastrophies sending human beings to unknown worlds; but the type of men and women they picture are pathetically like people of our chaotic society, little people with small desires, eager to play golf on ever more distant moons or planets. Has our modern technology produced more Buddha-like and Christ-like individuals, or even more all-embracing minds than Plato or da Vinci? Has it not rather assembly-built more cleverly engineered puppets able to gesticulate more freely and frantically under the direction of soulless puppeteers whose brains are webs of quantitative values, even if trained to repeat endlessly noble slogans and glamour-infused verbiage?

Yet crises can be furnaces in which the coal of ego-structured desires is transmuted into glowing diamonds. Are you willing to accept the processs of catharsis and metamorphosis because of the possiblity of emerging as the "Diamond soul" of which Buddhism speaks? Risk is involved. He who enteres upon "the Path of discipleship" wages his life or his sanity on the long-to-be-sustained operation. The purification of desire and the steeling of the essential Will — deep below the mere ego-will — are not easy processes. Not only work, but utterly dedicated work — not only service but irrevocably consecrated service — are needed. Strength, courage, inner stillness, an unemotional and unglamorized type of devotion are called for. Can you accept that they are needed? Are you willing to let the *quality* of your dedication be tested, tested again and again?

These are all questions which are involved in experiences related to your natal sixth house. Again the issue rests upon *how* you are approaching and formulating the everyday living of answers to these questions. Your natural and temperamental approach may be a Martain kind of impetuosity or a Venusian eagerness to determine and to feel vividly the value of every step. You may pour solar vitality and will into your dedication, or pass much time looking for a Hindu guru (Jupiter) or an expert in some technical skill able to set down for you specific steps in a formal training (Saturn). You may react intuitively to the momentum of social changes and the challenge of new worlds (trans-Saturnian planets). You may place your trust in your innate capacity for immediate and spontaneous feeling-adjustment to changes (the Moon), or in your ability to ascertain intellectually the character of every phase of the crisis of transformation and its relationship to other phases so that you may never lose the "Ariadne thread" which will guide you through the maze of conflicting ideas and fallacious claims (Mercury).

Whatever you are able, willing and ready to use should be understood to be merely a tool. Man creates myriads of tools. Alas, he may now become, and perhaps he has also been in long past eras, the servant of the very tools he has created. This perhaps is the crisis behind all more obvious crises which we are today facing — or trying to elude.

I and Thou — But Not Alone

Selfhood and relationship are the two polarities of all individualized existence. The individual remains what he is at the very core of his being through the unceasing changes which result from almost infinitely varied kinds of relationships. But what underlies all changes is not the ego, which is merely a more or less formalized and rigid set of responses to everyday encounters, but the silent and steady power of the self, the fundamental rhythm and archetypical form of the individuality. What today is often misnamed "the self" is *the person,* the total being; both physical and psychic. Within that person a constant interaction between the self and the Other occurs, and consciousness is the product — and in a metaphysical sense, also the source of such an interplay. Likewise *Yang* and *Yin* constantly interact within the great symbol of Chinese wisdom, the *Tai Chi.*

This interaction in its phase of greatest intensity is love, the I-Thou relationship sung alike by philosoper-mystics and poets. But love is a word of most varied meanings, and what crimes, what mad possessiveness, what jealous frenzy have not been experienced in the name of love! Everything in the personal and social-religious life of man depends upon the quality of the love-relationship. It is an exclusive relationship which keeps out all but the two emotionally bound participants, or is it a foundation which sustains, gives strength and thus, in one way or another, includes a complex web of interpersonal associations?

Why should the at least relatively permanent love-relationship — whether or not sanctified by law, church and custom — include more than the "I and Thou"? Because I and Thou are never alone; because no relationship has essential meaning except in

126

terms of some greater Whole in which it occurs. Not only any true marriage, but any essentially legitimate and sound partnership at the social, cultural and business level, should be defined by what it intends to bring to the community of mankind. It is to this end that the expectable transformation which the relationship produces in the partners should be given meaning. The Two should come together so that by allowing their union to introduce a new dimension and a new quality of being into their respective acts, feelings and thoughts they may jointly participate more significantly and constructively in the community.

It should be clear that this term, community, may be interpreted at several levels. It may mean a tribal type of family, a closely-knit Medieval or old New England village, a nation or even an invisible and mystical community, the ideal of which has been expressed in the, alas, so often grossly materialized concept of the White Lodge. At any level it refers to a widely inclusive whole within which two or several partners consciously realize themselves participating units.

It is this participation — implicit perhaps at first, then becoming increasingly explicited as the relationship unfolds — which gives to the relationship its truly spiritual quality. A love that merely joins two polarized halves to reconstitute some undifferentiated original state of unity can hardly be called spiritual, however beautiful it may be, however passionate and total its embraces. The goal of evolution is NOT to return to an undifferentiated primordial state of unity — the great dream of pseudo-mystics! — but to reach, together with many other beings a condition of unanimous, but still individualized, consciousness; what I have called the "multi-une" state of the Pleroma, the Omega state of being.

This is the human destiny. This is the ultimate goal. Two persons may walk hand in hand, heart beating with heart, in a rhythmic antiphony of love; but it is the walking toward the untimate state that gives to their love their functional value as well as their truly ecstatic purpose.

127

Meditate on that quality of love, my friends; for without it there can be no spiritual community, not even any truly "new" Age, whether of Aquarius or any other sign. Try to discover within your deepest nature the path to that love. It is not only "sharing" that matters, it is the quality and purpose of the sharing. Young people today place so much hope in the word, love; but theirs is often such a naive hope, because the very ideal of love is not tested against the reality of the drives of the biological and emotional nature. It is an "out of gears" state in which nothing happens that is truly spiritual because it is not related to the next step ahead in human evolution. It can thus become a state of emotional self-indulgence, or of indulgence in the Other. It may be beautiful, yet barren of transformation in depth, because it is "fire by friction," but not "solar fire" — to use occult terms.

In order to be a sun, one has to belong to the galactic Brotherhood of stars. True love aspires not only to a transsendence of the ego, but to a transcending of love in a mystic communion with the universe. Even the love of the devotee for his God must be transcended, if divinity, as a state of consciousness and being, is to be reached.

In the search for the meaning of love and the transmutation of possessiveness and self-centeredness, the Descendant of one's birth-chart can give a significant clue. Planets in the seventh house often can show the way out of problems and tensions arising from close associations. Several planets in this section of the Western sky at birth should suggest that a variety of experiences is needed to come to terms with a too dominant yearning for intimate relationship; a yearning which presupposes some inner insecurity and perhaps the need to overcome individual price or egocentricity. Always however in considering the Descendant one should relate it to the Midheaven; for it is at the Midheaven that what has *begun* in relationship comes to maturity in one's actual capacity to participate effectively in the community one has chosen, or which birth has imposed. It may begin in sweetness, in passion, in ecstasy, in great hopes; but the fruits may be bitter if the circumference of love proved to be a shell.

128

Rituals of Social Togetherness

Any relationship which as a character of at least relative stability generates energy. It produces also new needs. If the relationship is open and involves other lives it tends to expand. It relates itself to other relationships, and this second and more complex level of relationship generates a field of interpersonal, and eventually intergroup activities which tend to assume some regular form. Patterns of associations are constituted which, as they perpetuate themselves, produce what we call a "society."

At the core of, and pervading any type of social organization one finds always a fundamental, even if mostly implicit, purpose. A collective need is being met. A particular rhythm of togetherness emerges out of all encounters which settle into stable relationships — a quality of living which undertones the varied modes of everyday existence displayed by such relationships.

The formation of a society is a ritualizing process, however loose the patterns of the ritual may be. Ritualization begins in the home of couples and families. The process spreads widely as the field of associative activities expands and includes more varied types of participants with more imaginative and more individualized desires — and later on more obsessions and psychological complexes.

Three great steps are evident in the ritualizing process. At first we witness the attempt at interpersonal adjustment through *feelings* and through a realization of common needs and interests, above and beyond personal urges and impulses. Then, as society grows in complexity, *mental processes* come to the fore when men search for general principles underlying personal and group motives. When they think they have discovered such principles they devise laws and philosophies in order to increase the effectiveness and stability of the activities of the group.

Finally as the impulses of passionate and egocentric individuals often inevitably run counter to these laws, sanctions have to be established. Sanctions imply *collective actions* taken by the social whole against an individual part whose activities — and even at times, motivating feelings and thoughts — challenge the social sense of right or ritual. This social whole may be the tribe, the family, the State, or even the universe, for the universe also is understood to operate according to natural laws, or according to the will of an all-powerful God.

These three steps, involving feelings, mental processes and the operation of sanctions correspond to the eighth, ninth and tenth houses of a birth-chart. The foundations which determine the character of this entire process are the quality and the implied purpose of seventh house relationships.

The traditional and popularized meaning attributed to the eighth house — death, legacy, regeneration — makes very little sense, when considered in relation to the meanings of the opposite house (the second) or of the preceding seventh house. This section of the birth-chart refers rather to the change in feeling which can and should transform the individual as he finds himself involved in the many rituals of his society — and first of all in those types of joint activities which result from his relationship with his intimate partners. In this sense only can the eighth house symbolize a process of at least potential "re-birth." The essential point is that what is at stake is a change in *feelings*.

As a person enters into a more or less steady relationship with another person, or with associates in a social enterprise, the individual's basic feeling toward life in general tends to become altered — especially the feeling toward other human beings who have become at least theoretically his equals, his peers. If this transformation of feelings does not occur, then the relationship will sooner or later break down, turn unproductive. What is worse, it may become an instrument for the glorification of the ego — thus a negation of the true feeling of relationship.

A ritual is a well-defined form of activity through which a number of participants correlate and bind their energies in order to produce results which enhance their feeling of togetherness or group-identity. This is obviously the case where religious ritual or ceremonies are concerned. Even the complex rituals of the business world and the pattern of activity which can be seen through days and nights in the streets and buildings of a city are essentially means devised more or less deliberately to enhance the feeling of community.

At first what is involved is a community of interests and of desires. The participants seek to enjoy a more secure, more stimulating and fulfilling type of living. The vast increase in power which a society makes available to its members — unequal as the distribution of power may be — provides such benefits. If, in our modern technological world, these bring also a deep shadow, it is because the "coming together" of human beings is vitiated at root by greed and egocentric lust for power.

What we call today business is a materialistically organized form of religion. Both have their fanatic aspect. Religion worships a security-providing God at the emotional-psychic level; business worships Gold, as a symbol of personal and social power. Ceremonial magic is also a more occult form of power-worship.

Business rituals (for instance "markets" of all types and the power-game between labor and Management) can be productive of wealth and incentives for growth and social progress. Religious rituals become the foundations for a particular culture, inspiring creative minds, craftsmen and stabilizing institutions. Yet the nature of the results depends upon the quality of the relationships which generate the group-emotions and the deeply personal feelings of the participants in all such rituals.

Are you aware, clearly aware of *why* you participate in them? Is it a matter of conformity to a family and social norm, of habit, of taken-for-granted feeling-responses — or a conscious and deliberate readiness to share energies and profound experiences of togetherness with individuals in whom you trust and with whom you are willing to venture forth in a communion of feelings of faith and of hope?

Sex and Rites of Passage

The seventh house field of experience refers to the coming together of human beings. This coming together is always to some extent and in some manner related to a purpose. For archaic man the purpose was a pulling together of energy and skill to establish a relatively secure and stable community. Later on through marriage and business associations, the basic aim was to perpetuate and expand the culture and the radius of action of such a community. Today in our individualistic society individuals come together mainly in order to lead a richer, happier, more emotionally, mentally and perhaps spiritually fulfilling existence, often with little concern about what happens to society and the environment as long as the society and the environment provide them with what they want.

"Coming together" should lead to "feeling together"; and this is where the eighth house type of experience comes into the picture. At present this feeling-together is usually left to chance and outer circumstances; because of this so much goes wrong in our society. In older societies care was being taken to vividly impress upon the consciousness of the participants in a new type of relationship the importance and meaning of the step they were taking. This was done through what can be generally called "rites of passage."

Any change in interpersonal relationship was ritualized, and the ritual was meant to compel the person making the change to feel physically and emotionally as deeply as possible the *character* and *irreversibility* of the change. Puberty rites, marriage rites, maternity rites, and initiation rites are the best known of these ceremonies. These rituals, some of them very severe and death-defying, were meant to alter fundamentally the *feelings* of those who were beginning to operate at a new level of relationship within their well-integrated society.

It is in this light that one should consider the importance of the first sexual experience. A complete sexual relationship is the most fundamental means to give to those who have been drawn together by some kind of attractive force and often not at all clear purpose a feeling-in-depth — a totally involving feeling — of what interpersonal relationship can and should mean where love and a community of purpose or dedication prevails.

One speaks today of "sexual revolution." But the widespread permissiveness and the familiarity with nude bodies and their inter-action in sex-play or sensual responses prevalent today, at least in large sections of the country, constitutes only a *deconditioning* process. It is a reaction against the Christian ideal of life and in particular Puritanism. Very little about it is positive. The real sex-ual revolution is still ahead of us. It implies the "sacralization" of sex. This sacred approach to sex can hardly be experienced except in a radically different type of society which would give an alto-gether new meaning to both the individual person and interper-sonal relationships of all kinds.

This meaning should be at the same time individualized and impersonal. Instead, sexual contacts today are the results of per-sonal and psychological more than biological needs or com-pulsions; they rarely express an individualized approach to what is expected of, and gained in the experience. After having exper-ienced the inhibition of sex (thesis), then the vulgarization of sex (antithesis), mankind should now deliberately approach sex as a "sacred" function consciously intent upon the transformation in depth of the participants. Such a transformation would lead to a basic change in the quality of *all* relationships. In spite of our pre-vailing social attitude, this change can and does occur today. Very often, however, it is a negative kind of change, for sex is rarely freed from either biological compulsion and psychological complexes, or both. There may be great moments of "sacrality" in the experience, but these are usually soon lost in the feeling of possessiveness, in traditional habit-patterns and in the clinging to what tend to be mainly an escape from boredom, inner emptiness, and often insecurity and fear.

What is needed is dispassion and objectivity — and the kind of impersonality which not only does not exclude individualized awareness and a conscious sense of purpose, but alone can overcome the pull of unconscious compulsions and standardized moral attitudes.

How to bring into action within the relationship the transforming power of creative imagination and faith in the results of the experience of harmonized rhythm is certainly worth meditating upon. The prerequisites are an unceasing watchfulness and the capacity to remain intensely awake to the character of the feelings during and after the experience of relationship — of *any* relationshp in which feelings are involved. The value of rituals is that, if they are significantly performed, they demand the conscious use of imagination and a sharing in depth not only of feelings but of psychic being.

In many ancient rites of puberty the adolescent experienced sex as a sacred function in which the whole community, or at least its consecrated members were involved. The whole organism was being possessed by life-energies beyond any personal frame of reference. Likewise, the pure Tantrik rituals were based on the same super-personal approach to sex. To most modern individuals such experiences would be basically alien, yet there is something essential in the ideal which can be reactivated in terms of the new centering of human consciousness at the level of individualized consciousness.

In any case, to the person intent upon working out in his or her life the values revealed by astrological symbolism one thing should be clear: the eighth house of a birth-chart refers to the transformation in depth or transmutation which a relatively stable relationship between individuals can and should bring to the feeling-life of these individuals. The keywords of the house are: sharing and mutuality in an experience of relationship which as nearly as possible involves the whole person.

Problems Raised by Expansion

The phrase "expansion of consciousness" fascinates the mind of the youth stirred by T.V. and vast opportunities for travel and unfamiliar experiences, and disenchanted with the way of life and false standards of cities and suburbia. In fact, our entire Western civilization, especially since the fourteenth century has been geared to the drive for "more and more," to the quest for a "beyond" which promises a vaster field of experience, greater wealth at one level or another, and thus a more abundant life.

It is the nature of all living organisms to seek wider fields of activity, which usually implies the conquest of whatever occupies their immediate surroundings. But in the Western world, and particularly in America, the drive for material conquest has taken an unusually critical form. It has included the conquest of entities which normally keep the population within definite limits allowing for a harmonic relationship with the environment as a whole. The issue which confronts mankind is now clear: Is our goal to produce *bigger men,* or *more-than men*? Should we seek expansion or transcendence?

A crucial question. It has to be solved, symbolically speaking, in the ninth house of our chart. It must be solved through a clear mental awareness of what is involved in the choice.

The mind usually operates along the path outlined by the basic quality of our interpersonal relationship and by the depth of our feeling-experiences in relationship. Nevertheless the mind can function at its own level and in relative independence from actions and feelings. It does so because, when clearly or vividly formulated, thoughts can deal with conditions which transcend time, place and local relationships. Mind can operate in the realm of "universals." It extracts principles and laws from events and experiences studied objectively by groups and generations of experiencers. Generalized and absract statements transcend "particulars," i.e., personal, temporary and localized experiences. Moreover mind may also be able to *resonate* to the consciousness of beings whose fields of existence are immensely larger than our own, limited as our consciousness is by bio-psychological factors and impediments. Such a process of resonance implies the possibility of what appears to be a "revelation." Man can contact in his mind and become the agent for spiritual beings that are more-than-men.

The *mind of transcendence* is rooted in inner-revelations; it is the mind of shamans, prophets, seers, inspired geniuses. The *mind of abstraction* is based on an at least relatively impersonal and objectivizing communication linking minds of one epoch, and those of successive generations, in a Universal Company of scientists and explorers of unknown realms.

Yet each of these two types of minds can become perverted by the lure of bigness and abundance. Quantitative increases in value take the place of qualitative transformations consecrated to the eventual attainment of a transcendent ability consciously to participate in the activity of a biology-transcending and unanimous Community of more-than-men. Ambition — for the individual person or as well for the group — polarizes consecration to a more-than-human purpose. One may dream of colonization, or of universalization.

Today relentless and insecure men are already planning to colonize planets in this or other solar systems, eager no doubt to bring them the "blessings" of our waste-loaded and neurotic civilization. In terms of its planetary life span mankind as a whole is probably living today through a period corresponding to the "change of life" in human beings. What is needed is not escapism, even if glamorized by technological achievements, but repolarization.

What is needed is a basic reversal of attitude, from quantity to quality, from ambition for power and greed for soul-stifling abundance, to a totally dedicated openness to the transcendent and the transforming. Such a dedication no doubt can backfire into glamour-laden obscurantism and fanaticism. The light of clear spiritual inspiration may break down into unconscious mediumship and a confused "speaking of tongues." But this cannot be avoided. It is the basic ninth house challenge.

Meditate upon the clues your ninth house may present. Do not be impressed by "benefic" planets in this house; they may hold you prisoner in a net of expansionism. Everything whether called fortunate of unfortunate, serves its purpose. What is important is to keep awake and objective, as one expands. Test and retest your intuitions, your "great dreams." Seek confirmations. *You* are the limits, not the sky.

The Way to Achievement

In America men traditionally worship achievement; but what does constitute true achievement? It is the actualization, within the limits more or less forcefully imposed by your constitution and your social and geographical environment, of a set of potentialities inherent in your birth situation — that is, in your fundamental relationship to the universe.

The process of actualization may have a quality and a goal which are not congruent with the traditional character and the normal aims of your society and its culture, or even of a particular group — ethnic, religious or intellectual. Each collectivity of men has a more or less well defined ideal of achievement, the image of which it tries to impress upon the consciousness of children and growing individuals. One can accept it or refuse to respond to it. Still the longing to achieve a definite position, the validity of which the group of one's peers can accept and appreciate, is inherent in most human beings, even if only in a negative sense — that is, as a subtly masochistic glorification of what one believes to be a deep-seated refusal to succeed.

The path to achievement begins at the Ascendant. It takes a more definite form at the Nadir. It is tested by the pressures of close relationships; and these relationships provide the substance needed for the achievements-in-the making — helping or hindering, sustaining, or dissolving the will to accomplish, as may be the case. Relatively permanent relationships like marriage or a stable business partnership "gear" the desire for achievement to a particular rhythm of group activity. This desire has to operate in terms of a more or less definite conception of what is valuable, i.e., what constitutes success. The individual character of the will to achieve

140

can therefore become adulterated or deviated by the subtle or crude impact of collective ideas and ideals of success. The immediate concrete needs of the relationship can do the adulterating; so can the special feelings generated by the practices or rituals of relationship — feelings which may arouse a kind of ambition and greed for power — *over* human beings.

What is at stake in your tenth house is the quality of the success and the nature of the power for which you are striving. Is it success in terms of the actualization of your innate potential of being, your true individuality — or success measured by collective social-cultural standards of value? Your life may be dedicated to change or destroy these standards, and you may be successful in your efforts, but this still means that collective values direct your line of achievement. You are bound by them just because your achievement is to destroy them.

It may be that it is your individual destiny to take such a revolutionary line of action, and if so your tenth house and its cusp (Zenith point) may show what you will have to fight against. Saturn in that house will stress the potential strength of ego-will in its drive toward success, but also the incapacity of the ego to open itself to a transcendent purpose which would require ego-surrender. Because of this, success may lead to a sense of futility and a failure of the will, even though the individual may still keep on making the old gestures which brought success, but in the end can only lead to failure.

The Sabian symbol for the Midheaven degree may well be worth meditating upon;* but there is very often the possibility that this degree may not be correct. It has in any case to be considered in relation to those of the other three Angles of the chart. What is

---

*The original formulation and Marc Jones' interpretation of these symbols — which I merely condensed in my book THE ASTROLOGY OF PERSONALITY — leaves much to be desired for meditative purposes. I therefore prepared a complete reformulation of these symbols stressing their deeper value and complex interconnections in my book AN ASTROLOGICAL MANDALA, Random House, New York 1974.

important is not whether or not a man reaches what his society calls success, but the *quality of his reaching;* and this essentially means how much of his true individual selfhood he focuses into his public, social or professional endeavors.

Every individual has his or her true "vocation." He or she is called upon to *perform* on the stage of mankind, according to the form of his or her innermost nature. The birth-chart may not tell what the performance *will* be and whether or not it can be called successful in the eyes of other human beings; but it should give us significant clues concerning what is involved in our reaching whatever we do reach — provided we keep in mind the whole picture and do not become excited by the presence of this or that planet in the tenth house and by its so-called fortunate or unfortunate aspects.

Among several factors worth studying and meditating upon are the nature and position of the planet traditionally ruling the sign at the Midheaven. This planet may have much to do with the type of activity which it is best for you to emphasize as you move along the path to achievement. The life-function symbolized by that planet can become the basic source from which to draw as you seek to gain the power necessary for the accomplishment of your life-task. If this planet is in tense aspect to the ruler of the Descendant, but in harmonic aspect to that of the Ascendant — or vice versa — you may see from this whether the use of the originating power of your individuality, or a steady reliance upon what you may derive from close interpersonal relationships is more to be stressed in the fulfillment of your true vocation.

Ideals and Escapes

What do we really mean when we say that a person has reached "maturity"? What is the difference between an immature and a mature person? Most people would find it difficult to give a clear answer to these questions. One answer might be that a mature person has learnt to face reality, to come to grips with things as they are, instead of believing that they conform to the picture of what we imagine or want them to be. Yet the pictures of the world and of ourselves which we have in our minds are pre-determined by our culture, our language, our family or national tradition. As children we are made to see in a specific manner what we are told is reality. We substitute conceptual images of what a house, a man, a well-dressed person are for our direct and imme-diate sense-experiences of them.

It is natural for many a youth to resist the forceful or subtle impact of the models of perception, feeling and behavior to which they are urged to conform. The middle-aged man or woman who has lived to know how powerful and binding these impacts are may also refuse to accept any longer their validity. Whether young or old, there are individuals who at all times seek to build un-conventional images of reality and to challenge the *status quo* in their own consciousness and/or in society. Driven by discontent and a passion for change they may fight "the system" in the name of an ideal wherever they operate as members of a community, a class, a profession.

We speak of some of these men and women, perhaps with ad-miration, as reformers, prophets, innovators of genius, or with a mixture of fear and outrage, as radicals and revolutionists. Are they mature or immature persons? They can be either. What makes the difference is their inner attitude and the reasons for which they seek to transform or destroy the image of reality normally held by the people of their society. The basic issue is whether the new (or revitalized) images of themselves and of the world which have given a new direction to their emotions and/or to their thinking processes can be considered to be "ideals" or rather modes of "escape."

The variety of life-experiences which can be classified under the heading of eleventh house experiences fall into three basic categories defined by our attitude toward reality, as our culture and society see reality. We can enjoy what society and our social-professional achievements have brought to us. We can be impelled to try to change partially or totally the system, the workings of which stirred in us discontent, scorn, disgust or violent revulsion. We can also withdraw from this social reality in a world of dreams, fancy, illusion, self-deceit, and even of masochistic enjoyment of failure.

The rebel driven by his sense of injustice, his sufferings, his frustrations or despair does not lose contact with "reality" *if* his struggle is polarized by definite ideals which at least he believes workable and eventually actualizeable. He confronts one kind of reality with another. . . unless his struggle is intrinsically colored by personal immaturity, unless it is a form of escape. Idealism can indeed be a screen for escapism. Because one has not the courage, patience and persistence needed to understand and accept what steady relationships may demand, it is easy to consider them too inadequate and invalid to bother with. A dream-situation conjured in the emotional or over-sensitive mind by a mixture of hope, fear and imprecise longings is substituted for the real situation.

What constitutes escapism is the *substitution* of the imaginary for the real. One may most validly hold in consciousness an ideal of what a relationship should be and perhaps can become. One may visualize this ideal situation and try to understand clearly what it would imply if actualized. The real situation may be too different from what one visualizes to make an immediate attempt

144

at transformation possible or expedient. It may be too soon to think of definite ways in which this transformation could successfully occur. Thus the ideal may have to remain only an ideal, which other people may brush off by calling it "utopia." Still it is an ideal and not an escape, if the contrast between the ideal and the real is clearly understood, evaluated and accepted; and if whatever action can be taken which might lead to the actualization of the ideal is indeed performed, objectively and without unnecessary or dangerous illusions as to its effectiveness.

These considerations are worth meditating upon in our present period of wholesale crisis. Your eleventh house and its contents should alert you to the possiblity of self-deception or impatient rushing ahead in emotional impulses, whether they be aroused by personal immaturity or by the contagion of mass-excitement and fashion-induced moods of rebellion.

The Emptiness of Abundance

A time may come in life when after long and hard strivings toward certain types of achievements the fruits of so many endeavors rapidly materialize. Abundance succeeds scarcity; fulfillment replaces frustration. Perhaps suddenly and unexpectedly, what one has sown produces a rich harvest.

This can be a very significant spiritual test for the individual — a test of character and clarity of mind; a testing of the essential quality of the innermost being and feelings of the person. Men can be defeated by success and abundance even more than by failure or barrenness. What does one do with the rich harvest? How does one behave, feel and think under the pressures produced by the availability of that power, wealth or prestige for the attainment of which one may have so diligently and stubbornly struggled?

The type of power which is based on the ability to use the energy released by social processes as one's will and imagination dictate is generated in the tenth house; but it is in the twelfth house, symbolically speaking, that one has definitely to meet what this power has brought to oneself, both directly and indirectly through the reaction of society to the way the power has been used. For this reason the twelfth house has been called the house of karma.

Karma is often defined by the phrase: As you sow, so you shall reap. But this is an over-simplified concept. You may sow diligently and in the best manner possible, yet a drought or a tornado may destroy the expectable crop. An individual does not exist in a vacuum. He is a small component within a vast universe, or in more practical terms within an ecological and social whole. It is

146

not only what he does that matters, but as well how others act toward him and in response to what he has done. He is born at a particular time and in a particular locality within a community of human beings. This time-space equation — his birth-chart — sets definite limits to what he can achieve and what he can reap. His entire life is rooted in a particular set of potentialities. The real issue is how fully the individual is able to actualize at least a large number of these potentialities.

The issue is one of quality rather than of quantity. A poor peasant in Asia may have the richest kind of life. A tensely working American businessman who, driven by the worship of material success characteristic of his society, has sacrificed everything to the achievement of wealth and power may find in abundance only emptiness and boredom. In the eleventh house a man theoretically meets his ideals in a realized form, in the shape of friends, cultural and social enjoyment. Then what? What *meaning* do you give to what you have so long wanted, perhaps lacked and now possess in abundance? What is the quality of your enjoyment; or if you are a rebel who tried in vain to force his ideal upon social institutions and traditions full of inertia, how do you take your failure?

It is often very difficult to make a significant, vivid, long-to-be remembered ending to a cycle of experience — be it a relatively short end like a seven-year cycle, or your entire life span. A drama, a book, a symphony, a speech often drag on repetitively or confusedly before reaching a very flat or banal ending. The lives of our millions of retired "elderly citizens" have most of the time such a deeply meaningless, empty quality. Is it not better to die of heart failure in the ultimate exhaustion of vital and mental energies which have been used to the full for the actualization of one's birth-potential — perhaps in a supreme act of sacrifice to one's ideal, whatever it be?

What should never be forgotten is that the end of a cycle also releases the seed that will be the foundation for a new cycle. Death is a prelude to new life. Any truly great ending opens the gate to new and greater future experiences. Its majestic significance must not only fill the individual experiencing or witnessing it with a sense of fulfillment; it should evoke a deeper, more crucial feeling of emptiness, so that more life, God Himself, may find room for new birth. The greater the sense of plenitude the more total should be the longing for emptiness. Only the empty cup can be filled. Paradoxically our twelfth house should reveal to us both the character of our cyclic harvests and the way to relinquish abundance, that once more we may begin to reenter the field of existence, totally refreshed, totally renewed.

One Can Always Begin Again

The reader would miss the central point in our outlining of themes for meditation based on the "wheel of houses" if he or she did not realize that the twelve categories of individual experiences to which the houses refer exist simultaneously, in potentiality if not in clear-cut actuality. The twelvefold sequence constitutes an organic whole in terms of the gradual development of personality; but the chart should be understood and visualized in its reality beyond time as a *mandala*. It is the blueprint of our individuality.

These blueprints or *gestalt* of biopsychic activities are the universe's (or God's) way of communicating to our consciousness, individualized in a body-field of energies, the essential nature of our function on this planet, Earth, and clues as to how we can make the most of our many experiences. The cross of natal horizon and meridian, symbolizing the great dialogue of consciousness and power within us, is operative at every moment of our life, even if only one of its branches focuses our attention at a particular moment. Every phase of a cycle is contained implicitly in every other phase, the succeeding as well as the preceding phases. To be truly conscious is to be aware not only of the ever-shifting present moment, but of the place and function which the experiences it brings have in the entire cyclic process. Only an "eonic" consciousness able to embrace the structural pattern and ultimate purpose of the cyclic process as a whole can be said to operate in an Eternal Now.

In this Eternal Now birth and death are inseparably welded, as consciousness is integrated with power and selfhood with relatedness — I and the Other. The whole structure of the potentiality of individualized existence is implied at every point of the process of existence. Potentiality and actuality are the two poles of that process, and what the metaphysician calls non-being or non-manifestation is simply a state in which potentiality overwhelms actuality, and the cosmic Yin has reduced Yang to a condition of extreme latency.

Death and birth are likewise two critical moments of all existential and cyclic processes. Any ending should be seen also as a womb holding a potential beginning in its folds; and the ovum of tomorrow is always pierced by the spear of time, operating as karma. To say that one can always begin again is not the whole truth. One *must* always begin again, however distant the phase of however vast a cycle will unavoidably call for rebeginning.

What will begin again in a sense is "You"; yet in a more profound and cosmic sense it is rather a particular phase of cyclic existence, expressed in a totally new cosmic set-up, yet conditioned by what it has been as "You" in the far distant past. Every spring is a new spring bringing out new flowers. Yet all springs represent the same phase of a yearly cycle, and flowers reappear with the same biological features. Are they *the same* flowers? Do the roses of all springs contain the same atoms and molecules? Does not the solar system move into new fields of space at every moment? What then is ever rightfully to be called "the same"?

One can always begin again, but what does "one" mean? What does I or You actually mean? There is only One; and even this One may only be just like spring — a repetitive phase of a forever moving universal tide; moving within Space in which, both infinite extension and the dimensionless mathematical point — being and non-being — are harmonized.

Let us therefore rather say: Let there be always beginning! Indeed, there is always ending and beginning. Where they fuse, this mystery we call death is revealed in terms of future rebirth. This mystery, in astrological symbolism, is the Ascendant. At this point death and birth are one — and "You" are their embrace.

By DANE RUDHYAR

Art, Music, Philosophy

Claude Debussy et son oevre
Art As Release of Power
Beyond Individualism
Culture, Crisis and Creativity
Directives for New Life
Fire Out of the Stone
Occult Preparations For a New Age
Of Vibrancy and Peace
Paths to Fire
The Faith That Gives Meaning To Victory

The Magic of Tone and the Art of Music
* The Planetarization of Consciousness
Rania
Rebirth of Hindu Music
Return From No Return
The Rhythm of Human Fulfillment
The Rhythm of Wholeness
We Can Begin Again --- Together
White Thunder

Astrology & Psychology

*Astrological Aspects, A Process Oriented Approach
The Astrological Houses
*Astrological Insights Into the Spiritual Life
An Astrological Mandala
Astrological Signs
An Astrological Study of Psychological Complexes
Astrological Timing
*An Astrological Tryptich
Astrology and the Modern Psyche
The Astrology of America's Destiny
*The Astrology of Personality
*The Astrology of Transformation (Aurora distributes)
From Humanistic to Transpersonal Astrology
*The Galactic Dimension of Astrology
*The Lunation Cycle
New Mansions for New Men
*Person Centered Astrology
The Practice of Astrology

* Indicates a title published by Aurora Press

THE PLANETARIZATION
OF CONSCIOUSNESS

THE PLANETARIZATION
OF CONSCIOUSNESS

This is Rudhyar's major philosophical and psychological work, the concentrated outcome of a lifetime concerned with the most basic problems of human existence and the meaning of radical social-cultural crisis mankind is experiencing. Rudhyar has been for years an apostle of world integration based on the interpretation of Eastern and Western concepts and attitudes to life. He sees emerging a global society, and through the world-wide interaction of all cultures, a new type of "planetary" consciousness which for the first time will reveal in its fullness the potential of man.

"The holistic world-view which I present here is meant to be an incentive to think greater thoughts, to feel deeper, more inclusive feelings, and to act as "agents" for the Power that structures human evolution—however we wish to image this power."

RUDHYAR

The Planetarization is essentially an act of faith in Man. Man as a microcosm of the universe. Man as a reality that transcends the physical organism, all localisms and nationalisms, and in whom spirit and matter can unite in a "Divine Marriage" productive of ever new and greater creative tomorrows.

"I am particularly pleased because Rudhyar's whole trend of thought is in the spirit of psychosynthesis. From different starting points and using a different terminology he arrives at the same basic conclusion on important issues such as: harmonizing the opposites in individuals and in society; the central importance of purpose; the need of a new humanistic psychology."

ROBERTO ASSAGIOLI

ISBN: 0-943358-16-7   Paperback   336 Pages $22.95

Aurora Press
publishes books designed to catalyze personal growth, balance and transformation

Other Titles Available by Dane Rudhyar

Astrological Aspects: A Process Oriented Approach (With Leyla Rael Rudhyar)

Astrological Insights Into the Spiritual Life

An Astrological Triptych

The Galactic Dimensions of Astrology

The Lunation Cycle

Person Centered Astrology

The Planetarization of Consciousness

Aurora Press distributes
Astrology of Transformation, A Multi-Level Approach

For a complete catalog of all Aurora Press titles, write to:

AURORA PRESS
P O Box 573
Santa Fe , NM 87504
Tel: 505-989-9804

AURORA PRESS

Aurora Press is devoted to pioneering books that catalyze personal growth, balance and transformation. Aurora makes available in a digestible format, an innovative synthesis of ancient wisdom with twentieth century resources, integrating esoteric knowledge and daily life.

Recent titles include:

COMING HOME
Deborah Duda

CRYSTAL ENLIGHTENMENT
Katrina Raphaell

CRYSTAL HEALING
Katrina Raphaell

SILVER DENTAL FILLINGS • THE TOXIC TIMEBOMB
Sam Ziff

AWAKEN HEALING ENERGY THROUGH THE TAO
Mantak Chia

TAOIST SECRETS OF LOVE
Mantak Chia

THE LUNATION CYCLE
Dane Rudhyar

SELF HEALING, YOGA AND DESTINY
Elisabeth Haich

For a complete catalog write:

AURORA PRESS
P.O. BOX 573
SANTA FE NEW MEXICO 87504
Fax 505 982-8321
Email:Aurorep@aol.com